BASIC PROGRAMMING

BASIC PROGRAMMING

Paul W. Murrill   and   Cecil L. Smith

Louisiana State University
Baton Rouge

Intext
HARPER & ROW, PUBLISHERS
New York   Hagerstown   San Francisco   London

BASIC PROGRAMMING

Library of Congress Catalog Card Number: 78-143623
ISBN 0-700-22340-1

To Andy

PREFACE

The primary objective of this book is to serve as an introductory text on BASIC programming. This book and a minor amount of supplementary material on such aspects as the specific sign-on procedure for the computer system to be used should be sufficient for an introductory course on BASIC programming. This book does not assume any prior programming experience in Fortran, COBOL, PL/1, or other programming language.

Each chapter is supplemented with an extensive set of exercises on which the student can test his ability to use the BASIC language. Most of the problems require little mathematics background, and can be comprehended by a college freshman or even a senior high school student. Although BASIC is attractive to students at this level because of its simplicity, the language is equally useful on far more complicated problems. Therefore, a few exercises requiring a knowledge of higher mathematics have been included for the advanced student learning BASIC.

The subject matter in this text is arranged so that the student quickly begins to write programs, specifically, in Chapter 2. Subsequent chapters cover the more advanced features of BASIC in an orderly fashion, permitting the student to progressively prepare more complicated programs.

The authors wish to express special thanks to Professor Mary McCammon, Department of Mathematics, Pennsylvania State University, for her valuable suggestions for improving the manuscript. And we must express our appreciation to Mrs. Sonja Hartley, who typed and proofread the entire manuscript.

Paul W. Murrill
Cecil L. Smith

Baton Rouge, Louisiana
February, 1971

CONTENTS

BASIC PROGRAMMING

Chapter 1

INTRODUCTION TO DIGITAL COMPUTERS

The steam engine and other devices for doing work gave man an extension of his physical capabilities and brought about the Industrial Revolution. In a very similar manner, electronic computers are providing man with tools with which he can process quantities of information and solve problems that otherwise would be impossible to handle. These computers are producing an *information revolution* that will have more impact on each of our everyday lives than any other aspect of modern technology—even atomic energy! The purpose of this book is to assist you, as a student in whatever field you are pursuing, in learning to utilize these computers in your day-to-day work.

1-1. Digital-Computer Characteristics

Modern electronic computers are of two basic types—digital and analog. The entire contents of this book are directed toward understanding and programming *digital computers*, and no attention is devoted to the study of analog computers or combinations of analog and digital computers (hybrid computers).

Digital computers can be appreciated best by first considering some of their characteristics. Understanding these characteristics will help us to appreciate their usefulness.

One of the most prominent characteristics of digital computers is their truly incredible *speed*. Although they only work one step at a time, i.e., *sequentially*, they perform their tasks at rates that are beyond the comprehension of the novice. As an example, some large machines are capable of adding together several hundred thousand 16-digit numbers in less than a second of time! These tremendous speeds make it possible for the machine to do work in a few minutes that might otherwise require years of time.

Not only is the digital computer capable of working very rapidly, but it also has a perfect *memory*. It has virtually instantaneous "recall" of both data and instructions that are stored within itself, and it never forgets or loses the accuracy of the information which it has within its memory.

A digital computer is an extremely *accurate* device. In most machines numbers are handled with seven, eight, or nine significant digits, and twice this accuracy can usually be obtained by the programmer. This means that a machine would not hesitate to multiply 2782.4362 by 40.127896, obtaining the product correct to eight or sixteen significant figures.

Coupled with the significant characteristics already listed, the digital computer does its work *automatically*. It can accept instructions from its operator, then execute these instructions without need for human intervention. This implies that the machine can be given a problem and, while you attend a movie or play a round of bridge, will do your work with incredible accuracy and at fantastic speeds. Learning to use such a tool should require no further motivation.

1-2. Programming the Digital Computer

The digital computer is basically a device to accept *data* (in the form of numbers, alphabetic characters, or symbols) and a set of instructions as to how to manipulate these data in order to produce a set of answers (in the form of numbers). The set of instructions is called the *program*, and these are prepared by a *programmer* (you). (See Fig. 1-1.) This book is primarily concerned with the prep-

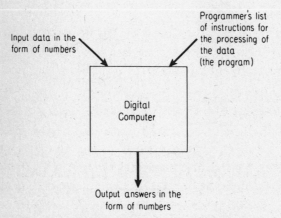

Fig. 1-1. Functional role of the digital computer.

aration of programs. Sometimes the data may be contained within the program; sometimes the data are entered into the computer after the program.

The primary concern of this manual is not how the computer works, but how to tell the computer to do what you want it to do—in other words, how to prepare a *computer program*.

Basically, the computer can only perform a certain number of instructions; for example, to add one number to another; to determine if a number is positive, negative, or zero; and so on. At the lowest level, these instructions consist of a pattern of ones and zeros which the computer understands perfectly well but which can be interpreted by humans with difficulty and only after working with the machine for an extended period of time. Programming at this level is said to be in *machine language*, and is avoided whenever possible for obvious reasons.

One step up the ladder is *assembly language*, which permits the use of mnemonics for the instructions. Programming at this level is still tedious, but can be justified for many purposes that require access to the basic capabilities of the computer. Programs prepared at this level will also execute, i.e., produce answers, faster than those prepared at higher levels. However, the assembly language is specific to a given machine, and programming at this level is far too tedious and time-consuming to be considered by most users.

The next step up the ladder brings us to the procedural languages. A number of these have appeared, each designed to be attractive to a given class of users whose needs distinguish them from another set. The more notable of these languages are:

1. COBOL, a language specifically designed to meet the needs of users in the field of business.
2. FORTRAN, a language used primarily by those in the scientific area but general enough to find applications in practically all areas.
3. ALGOL, a competitor to FORTRAN. ALGOL was received much better in Europe than in the United States.
4. PL/1, or Programming Language One, a language that combines the features of FORTRAN and COBOL.
5. BASIC, a language developed primarily for users of time-sharing systems. BASIC is by far the easiest of the languages to learn and to use.

BASIC, which stands for *B*eginner's *A*ll-Purpose *S*ymbolic *I*nstruction *C*ode, was originally developed at Dartmouth College, Hanover, New Hampshire, for the GE 235 Time Sharing system, but has subsequently been extended to other GE systems and to systems of other manufacturers, including the XDS Sigma Series, IBM Time Sharing systems, PDP Time Sharing systems, and a number of others.

By "time sharing systems" we mean computer systems whose time is shared by several different users via teletypes. Due to the computer's speed, each user can communicate with the computer as if he were the only user. Since the computer can communicate with the user over telephone lines, each user may be in a separate location several hundred miles from the computer.

1-3. An Introduction to BASIC

Although subsequent chapters will present a detailed development of the BASIC language, this section will begin the discussion of BASIC by presenting a simple example so that the reader can get some idea of what is to come.

Suppose we would like to compute the total pay of a salesman who receives a base pay plus commission. Suppose our chap receives $87.25 per week plus 4 percent commission on all sales over $100. We propose to write a program into which we can readily insert values of his base pay and his total sales for the week, obtaining his total pay.

```
10 READ B,S
20 IF S<100 THEN 50
30 LET C=0.04*(S-100)
40 GOTO 60
50 LET C=0
60 LET T=B+C
70 PRINT "TOTAL PAY IS" T
80 DATA 87.25,175.80
99999 END

>RUN
TOTAL PAY IS 90.282
```

Fig. 1-2. Simple program illustrating general features of the
BASIC program.

The computer program and corresponding output are shown in Fig. 1-2.‡ This program is practically self-explanatory, which is one of the attractive features of BASIC. If the program had been previously stored in the computer, the listing in Fig. 1-2 is obtained by instructing the computer to list the program. Note that each line in the program begins with a number (called the line number), which provides an easy mechanism by which to refer to lines in the program. The first line, i.e., line 10, instructs the computer to "read" values for variables B and S, which in the program represent the *base pay* and the *sales* for the week, respectively. These values are obtained from the **DATA** statement, which happens to be in line 80 in our program. Execution of the **READ** statement, causes the value 87.25 to be assigned to B and the value 175.80 to be assigned to S.

Following the **READ**, control is transferred to line 20, which determines if our man's sales for the week exceeds $100. If S is less than $100, then line 50 is executed to give him no commission for the week. If S is not less than (i.e., greater than or equal to) $100, line 30 is executed to compute his commission as 4 percent of sales in excess of $100. Line 40 is a **GOTO** statement that transfers control directly to line 60, which computes his total pay, T. The **PRINT** statement in line 70 writes the characters enclosed in the single quotation marks followed by the numerical value of T. The last statement in the program is the **END** statement, which terminates our program.

Following completion of listing the program, the computer then awaits instructions from the user. In our system, the computer types the "prompt" character < to indicate that it is ready to accept input. Upon entering **RUN**, the computer executes the program, giving the answer as illustrated in Fig. 1-2.

---

‡Note in line 40 of Fig. 1-2 that the letters "oh" in **GOTO** cannot be readily distinguished from the zeroes except by the context in which they are used. Some systems distinguish between these by placing a slash through the number zero, i.e., Ø, to distinguish it from the letter "oh," as is illustrated in Fig. 2-1 in the next chapter.

This convention depends upon the model of terminal available, and is by no means universal. In this text, slashes through the zero will appear only in some of the figures and in some of the solutions in Appendix C. Unfortunately, some systems use just the opposite convention, i.e., a slash through the "oh." This is never used in this text.

It is surprising how many useful programs can be prepared using just the simple statements illustrated in this example. However, BASIC is far more powerful than this, yet is able to retain much of its simplicity. It is a very attractive programming language for the beginning or occasional user of the computer who is interested in numerical answers to his problems rather than programming for the sake of programming. It also lends itself very nicely to users of terminals.

Chapter 2

SIMPLE PROGRAMS

The objective of this chapter is to present just enough features of BASIC to enable the student to prepare programs to do simple yet meaningful tasks for him. However, except for the READ and PRINT statements, the features that are presented will be developed in full.

2-1. Elements of a BASIC Program

This section presents six fundamental elements of the BASIC language that are found in virtually all BASIC programs. These elements are line numbers, constants, variables, arithmetic operators, expressions, and intrinsic functions.

Line numbers, also called *step numbers* or *statement numbers*. Each line in the basic program must begin with a unique line number containing five digits or less, i.e., from 1 to 99999. The computer executes the statements in the order specified by the line numbers.

Consecutive numbering of lines is not recommended, since it would be impossible to insert a new line without renumbering the remaining lines in the program. Note in the example in Fig. 1-2 that the lines were numbered in increments of ten, except for the END statement, which was given a line number 99999, the largest number permissible, since this statement will always be the last statement in the program.

The computer automatically reorders the statements according to their line numbers before executing them. Therefore, if a statement needs to be added to a program, it can be added at any point, say at the very end. Before executing the program, the computer will place it in its proper sequence according to its line number. Subsequent listings of the program will show the line in its appropriate position.

Constants, or numbers, are positive or negative numbers that normally contain up to seven digits or more‡ that either stand alone, have an embedded decimal point, or are preceded or followed by a decimal point. The following numbers would be acceptable as constants in a BASIC program:

‡This varies somewhat from machine to machine, GE permitting eleven.

$$19$$
$$.172$$
$$1.72$$
$$-979.$$
$$+.00276.$$

Unsigned numbers are assumed positive. An expression such as 16/3 is not a constant, but is composed of two constants (16 and 3), and would not be accepted as a constant in statements such as the **DATA** statement, the **DIM** statement, and other similar statements. Numbers containing more than seven digits, e.g., 123456789, are usually rounded. Leading zeroes used to indicate the position of the decimal point, for example, in 0.00001234567, are not counted.

Further flexibility is gained by using the *exponential notation* (also called *scientific notation* or *floating-point notation*), which consists of a number complying with the rules given above followed by the letter **E** and a two-digit exponent (which may be positive or negative but must not contain a decimal point). The **E** stands for "times ten to the power." For example, the constant **1.72E-4** is 1.72×10^{-4} or 0.000172. A negative exponent simply shifts the decimal point the prescribed number of places to the left, whereas a positive exponent shifts the decimal point to the right. The following entries are acceptable:

1.7E+4
1.7E4   (plus sign is optional)
.17E5
17E3   (note absence of decimal)
1E10

The last entry stands for "ten billion," and illustrates the fact that a number must precede the **E**. That is, simply **E10** would not be accepted.

A typical acceptable range of numerical values for both constants and variables within a BASIC program is from 10^{75} to 10^{-75} and zero, although this varies somewhat depending upon the specific model of computer.

Variables in BASIC are denoted by a letter of the alphabet, or by a letter of the alphabet followed by a digit from 0 through 9. This gives the programmer a total of 286 possibilities, which is generally sufficient. For example, the following variables are acceptable in BASIC:

A
B
X5
E2

Note that **E2** is a variable, not the constant 100. Unacceptable variables are:

AB   (too many letters)
X22   (too many digits follow-
            ing the letter)

Y*   (only letters and digits
            are permitted in variable
            names)
2X   (letter must precede digit)

Variables are given or "assigned" numerical values in statements such as READ, LET, and several others to be discussed in subsequent sections. The variable retains the value so assigned until encounter of another statement that assigns it a different value.

For example, consider the program in Fig. 2-1. The READ statement assigns

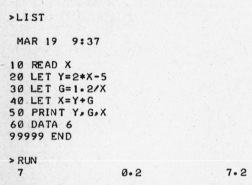

```
>LIST

  MAR 19   9:37

 10 READ X
 20 LET Y=2*X-5
 30 LET G=1.2/X
 40 LET X=Y+G
 50 PRINT Y,G,X
 60 DATA 6
99999 END

> RUN
 7                0.2              7.2
```

Fig. 2-1. Illustration of assignment of different
values to the variable X.

a value of 6 (as given in the DATA statement in line 60) to the variable X. This value is retained when lines 20 and 30 are executed. Line 40 assigns a new value to X, namely 7.2, which is the value printed in line 50.

The purpose of a variable is essentially to establish a storage location into which a number can be stored and retrieved by referring to the variable name. Whenever the numerical value of a quantity may change during execution of the program or from one run to the next, a variable must be used for this quantity.

Initially, all variables in a BASIC program are undefined, i.e., have not been assigned a value. We shall shortly examine several statements, e.g., LET and READ, by which a variable can be assigned a value, i.e., a numerical value is stored in the storage location reserved for the variable. It is imperative that the variable be assigned a value before the variable is used elsewhere in the program.

Arithmetic Operators. The basic mathematical operations are denoted in BASIC by the following symbols:

Symbol	Operation	Example	Explanation
+	Addition	A+B	A plus B
−	Subtraction	A−B	A minus B
−	Negation	−A	minus A
*	Multiplication	A*B	A times B
/	Division	A/B	A divided by B
↑ or **	Exponentiation	A↑B	A raised to the B power
		or A**B	

The upward arrow is the more popular symbol for exponentiation, and will be used throughout this book. Not all systems recognize the double asterisk.

In performing exponentiations, negative numbers (including variables whose value is less than zero) can be raised *only* to integer powers, the result being as if the number were multiplied by itself the prescribed integer number of times. If the exponent is not an integer, the operation A ↑ B is equivalent to

$$10 \uparrow [B \cdot \log_{10} A] \quad \text{or} \quad \exp [B \cdot \ln A]$$

Since the computer is unable to find the logarithm of a negative number, this operation is impossible whenever $A < 0$.

Expressions or Formulas. The symbols for arithmetic operations are used along with variables and constants to form expressions. Acceptable expressions are

$$A + B$$
$$A + 2$$
$$2/C$$
$$C * 2$$
$$C * 2 + B$$

An examination of the last entry indicates that this expression could indicate either (1) multiply C by 2 and add the result to B, i.e., (C*2) + B, or (2) add 2 to B and multiply the result by C, i.e., C*(2 + B).

This brings us to the order of precedence of the arithmetic operations, which is

Order of Precedence	Arithmetic Expression
1	↑ (exponentiation)
2	*,/ (multiplication and division)
3	+,− (addition, subtraction, and unary minus‡)

‡By a unary minus we mean the leading minus sign in expressions such as −A*(B+C).

According to this convention, the interpretation of the following expressions would be:

BASIC Expression	Algebraic Interpretation
C*2+B	$c * 2 + b$
C+B/2	$c + b/2$
C/2+B	$c/2 + b$
C↑2/D	c^2/d
−C↑2	$-(c^2)$, not $(-c)^2$

However, the expression A/B*C could mean either ac/b or a/bc and still comply with the order of precedence. This ambiguity can be resolved according to the following statement: "Operations on the same level of precedence are executed from left to right as they occur in the expression." The expression A/B*C would therefore be interpreted as "take A, divide by B, and multiply the result by C," making this expression equivalent to ac/b. Similarly, A−B−C is $(a - b) - c$ and A↑ B ↑ C is $(a^b)^c$, i.e., raise a to the b power and raise the result to the c power.

Parentheses may be used freely within an expression in much the same manner as in algebraic expressions to obtain the desired sequence of operations. Excess pairs of parentheses are permissible, so whenever the programmer is not sure of himself, he can safely add parentheses. There is no limit on the number of parentheses, but an expression must contain the same number of open and close parentheses. The following examples illustrate the use of parentheses:

BASIC Expression	Algebraic Interpretation
$((A+B)/C) \uparrow 2$	$\left(\dfrac{a+b}{c}\right)^2$
$X/(Y+2)$	$\dfrac{x}{y+2}$
$(A+B)/(Y+3)$	$\dfrac{a+b}{y+3}$
$((A+B)/(Y+3)) \uparrow (I+1)$	$\left(\dfrac{a+b}{y+3}\right)^{i+1}$

Mathematical Functions, or intrinsic functions. The mathematical functions in BASIC are given three letter names followed by an argument in parentheses. Table 2-1 lists the more commonly used functions that will be sufficient for our purposes in this text. A more complete list is given in Appendix A. These functions may occupy the same position in an expression as a variable or a constant can occupy. Furthermore, the argument X of the function may be a constant, a variable, or any valid expression. The following examples represent valid use of functions:

```
SQR( 4*Y+9 )
INT( A/B )
LOG( 10 )+Q
X+EXP( Y )
ABS( SIN( 4*G ) )
SQR( SQR( H ) )
```

The last example illustrates that functions may appear in an expression used as the argument of the same function or of another function.

The function **INT** essentially truncates, i.e., drops, the decimal part of a number.‡ That is, **INT**(4.717) is 4 and **INT**(−2.492) is −2. This function can be used for rounding to the nearest integer by simply adding 0.5 if the number is positive or by subtracting 0.5 if the number is negative. That is, the following statements provide rounding:

$$\text{INT}(X+.5) \quad \text{if } X \text{ is positive}$$

$$\text{INT}(X-.5) \quad \text{if } X \text{ is negative}$$

‡For some BASIC systems, this statement should read "the function **INT**(X) determines the largest integer number that does not exceed X." The two statements are equivalent for $X > 0$, but not for $X < 0$. For example, using this definition, **INT**(−2.492) is −3. The statement for rounding becomes **INT**(X + .5) for X positive or negative.

TABLE 2-1.   Common BASIC Functions

Function	Explanation
SIN (X)	Calculates trigonometric sine of X, where X is in radians
COS (X)	Calculates trigonometric cosine of X, where X is in radians
TAN (X)	Calculates trigonometric tangent of X, where X is in radians
ATN (X)	Calculates trigonometric arctangent of X. Result is in radians, and is positioned as follows: $$X < 0 \quad -\frac{\pi}{2} < \text{result} < 0$$ $$X \geq 0 \quad 0 \leq \text{result} < \frac{\pi}{2}$$
EXP (X)	Calculates the exponential function, e^x
LOG (X)	Calculates natural logarithm (base e) of X
LGT (X)‡	Calculates common logarithm (base 10) of X
ABS (X)	Calculates absolute value of X, $\mid X \mid$
SQR (X)	Calculates square root of X, $\sqrt{X}$
INT (X)	Calculates the integer part of X (See text for explanation.)
SGN (X)	Calculates the sign of X—that is, if $X < 0$ SGN $(X) = -1$ if $X = 0$ SGN $(X) = 0$ if $X > 0$ SGN $(X) = +1$

‡GE systems use CLG (X) in place of LGT (X) for the common logarithm.

If the values of X may change sign, the following alternative may be used:

INT(X+.5*SGN(X))

Similarly, the following modification rounds to the second decimal place:

INT(100*X+.5*SGN(X))/100

2-2. The LET Statement

The general form of the LET statement is as follows:

LET *variable* = *expression*

This statement causes the expression on the right of the equal sign to be calculated and the result assigned to the variable on the left of the equal sign.   Only *variables* may appear on the left of the equal sign. Valid examples of the LET statement are

```
10 LET Y=G
20 LET Z2=SQR(X4)-10
30 LET A9=4*A9-17
```

Note from the last example that the variable appearing on the left of the equal sign may also appear in the expression on the right of the equal sign. This is perfectly acceptable to the computer, and is executed as follows:

1. The expression is evaluated using the last value stored in A9 prior to execution of the current LET statement.
2. The result of the expression is assigned to the variable A9.

That is, for the above example, if the value of A9 prior to execution of the LET statement is 5, the value of A9 after execution is 3.

Note that the equal sign was *not* treated in the usual algebraic sense. In algebra, the statement

$$a_9 = 4a_9 - 17$$

is equivalent to

$$a_9 = \frac{17}{3} = 5.67$$

This is not the interpretation given by the computer. Instead, the equal sign more logically represents "replacement," that is, the value of A9 is replaced by the value of the expression on the right of the equal sign. By this interpretation, statements like

```
40    LET    J=J+1
```

make sense, simply causing the current value of J to be increased by 1.

Consider preparation of a program to compute the roots of an equation of the form

$$ax^2 + bx + c = 0$$

According to the quadratic formula, the roots are given by

$$r_{1,2} = \frac{-b \pm \sqrt{b^2 - 4ac}}{2a}$$

Knowing beforehand that the roots are real, the program in Fig. 2-2 will calculate the roots of the equation

$$x^2 + 3x + 2 = 0$$

Note the use of LET statements to define A, B, and C, calculate the value for the square root, and calculate the two roots. In the next section we will consider other statements that can be used to assign values to A, B, and C.

The student who is concerned about programming in the most efficient manner should note that execution of the expression B*B is somewhat faster than execution of the expression B↑2 used in line 40 of Fig. 2-2. The objective of the example was to illustrate as many features of BASIC as possible, and thus the use

```
>LIST

 MAR 18   8:57

10 LET A=1
20 LET B=3
30 LET C=2
40 LET R=SQR(B↑2-4*A*C)
50 LET R1=(-B+R)/(2*A)
60 LET R2=(-B-R)/(2*A)
70 PRINT R1,R2
99999 END

> RUN
-1                    -2
```

Fig. 2-2. Program to calculate
roots of a quadratic equation.

of $B \uparrow 2$. Perhaps this should not have been done, since students should be encouraged to follow good programming practices from the very start.

Recent versions of BASIC are liberalizing the **LET** statement to accept multiple assignments of the type

$$LET \quad A = B = C = D = 0$$

An expression may appear to the right of the last equal sign, but only variables may appear elsewhere. The user should check the manual for his system before using this feature to verify that it is supported. It is not used elsewhere in this text.

2-3. The READ and DATA Statements

The **READ** and **DATA** statements are used in conjunction to insert the appropriate numerical values to be used in execution of the BASIC program. The formats of the **READ** and **DATA** statements are as follows:

READ *variable, variable, variable, etc.*

DATA *constant, constant, constant, etc.*

Note that commas are used to separate the variables in the **READ** statement and to separate the constants in the **DATA** statement. However, no comma follows the word **READ** or the word **DATA**, nor does a comma follow the last variable or last constant in the respective list. Neither of these statements may appear in a BASIC program without at least one occurrence of the other statement.

The **READ** statement causes the variables listed in it to be assigned, in order, the next available values from the constants in the **DATA** statements. The **DATA** statements are scanned from left to right, top to bottom, in accordance with their line numbers. That is, the computer effectively considers all the **DATA** statements in the program to constitute one large data block. That is, the statements

```
100 DATA 1,2
110 DATA 3,4,5
120 DATA 6
```

are equivalent to the single statement

150 DATA 1,2,3,4,5,6

Although the **DATA** statements may occur anywhere in the program, they are usually placed just prior to the **END** statement so that (1) they will all be in one place for convenience and (2) to minimize renumbering of line numbers in case additional **DATA** statements are added to the program.

If the **DATA** block contains more constants than required by the **READ** statements, the excess constants are simply not used. However, if a **READ** statement contains more variables than the remaining constants in the **DATA** statement, an "out of data" message is printed and program execution is terminated.

Using the **READ** and **DATA** statements, the program in Fig. 2-2 to compute the roots of a quadratic equation can be modified to

```
10 READ A,B,C
20 LET R=SQR(B↑2-4*A*C)
30 R1=(-B+R)/(2*A)
40 R2=(-B-R)/(2*A)
50 PRINT R1,R2
60 DATA 1,3,2
99999 END
```

Changing the coefficients in the quadratic equation would require changing only the **DATA** statement in line 60 of the program, as opposed to changing the first three lines of the program in Fig. 2-2.

Note that multiple **READ** statements can be used with only one **DATA** statement, and vice versa. For example, the **READ** statements

```
10 READ A
15 READ B,C
```

could be used instead of the single **READ** statement in the above program to obtain the same result.

2-4. The INPUT Statement

For users of terminals, data may be entered into the program while it is running via the **INPUT** statement. The format of the **INPUT** statement parallels that of the **READ** statement, being

INPUT *variable, variable, etc.*

Rules for commas are also the same, being (1) no comma following the word **INPUT**, (2) separation of variables by commas, and (3) no comma after the last variable in the list.

Unlike the **READ** statement, no **DATA** statement is used with the **INPUT** statement. Instead, the values are entered by the user via the terminal. For example, the program in Fig. 2-3 illustrates the use of an **INPUT** statement in our program to calculate the roots of a quadratic equation.

```
>LIST

 MAR 18   9:18

10 INPUT A,B,C
20 LET R=SQR(B↑2-4*A*C)
30 R1=(-B+R)/(2*A)
40 R2=(-B-R)/(2*A)
50 PRINT R1,R2
99999 END

> RUN
?  1,3,2
-1                  -2
```

Fig. 2-3. Illustration of the use
of the **INPUT** statement.

Upon execution of the **INPUT** statement, the computer types the character **?** and waits for the user to enter the required values. These are entered on the same line, successive values being separated by a comma. After all values are entered, the user depresses the **RETURN** key and the computer proceeds with the rest of the calculations.

2-5. The PRINT Statement

The **PRINT** statement can be used to (1) print values of variables, (2) print the results of expressions, (3) print messages, and (4) skip a line.

Use of the **PRINT** statement to print values of variables has been used in several of the programs in previous examples. The format of the **PRINT** statement also parallels that of the **READ** statement, except that arithmetic expressions *or* variables may appear. The general form of the **PRINT** statement is:

> **PRINT** *arithmetic expression, arithmetic expression, etc.*

No comma follows the word **PRINT**; commas are used to separate the expressions; and no comma normally follows the last expression or variable. Exceptions to this last point along with other variations are discussed in Chapter 6 after the user is more familiar with BASIC.

Since expressions may be used in the place of variables in the **PRINT** statement, the program in Fig. 2-3 can be shortened to

```
10 INPUT A,B,C
20 LET R=SQR(B↑2-4*A*C)
30 PRINT (-B+R)/(2*A),(-B-R)/(2*A)
99999 END
```

Note the use of a comma to separate the two expressions. Of course, both expressions and variables may appear in the same **PRINT** statement.

Messages may also be used in place of variables or expressions in the **PRINT** statement. The message to be printed is enclosed in quotations, and is reproduced verbatim in the program's output. For example, the statement

```
20  PRINT "THE SQUARE ROOT OF "X, "IS" SQR(X)
```

gives the output (for $X = 4$):

THE SQUARE ROOT OF 4 IS 2

Note that no comma follows either of the last quotation marks in the above example. A comma may be used if desired, and will affect the appearance of the output. A line on the teletype is divided into five zones of fifteen spaces each. A comma causes the output to begin in the next print zone; or if the fifth print zone is filled, to move to the first print zone of the next line. Omission of a comma following the message (or more elegantly, alphanumeric information) causes the following data to be printed immediately.

In order to obtain headings, the alphanumeric information should be separated by commas. For example, the two **PRINT** statements

$$200 \quad \text{PRINT} \quad \text{"ROOT 1", "ROOT 2"}$$
$$210 \quad \text{PRINT} \quad \text{R1,R2}$$

would cause the headings **ROOT 1** and **ROOT 2** to be printed directly above the values of **R1** and **R2**. This will be illustrated shortly.

To obtain a blank line in the output, the statement

$$230 \quad \text{PRINT}$$

is used. Since there is no output to be transmitted, a blank line is obtained.

To illustrate these, Fig. 2-4 shows the use of **PRINT** statements to obtain head-

```
>LIST

 MAR 18   9:20

10 READ A,B,C
20 LET R=SQR(B↑2-4*A*C)
30 PRINT "A","B","C"
40 PRINT A,B,C
50 PRINT
60 PRINT "ROOT 1","ROOT 2"
70 PRINT (-B+R)/(2*A),(-B-R)/(2*A)
80 DATA 1,3,2
99999 END

> RUN
A                  B                  C
 1                  3                  2

ROOT 1             ROOT 2
-1                 -2
```

Fig. 2-4. Illustration of the use of **PRINT** statements.

ings and spacing in the output from our root-solving program. Note the commas separating the alphanumeric information to be used as headings.

2-6. The REM Statement

Explanatory remarks inserted at various points serve to make the program more understandable to the user as well as to others who may want to interpret it.

Examples of such remarks include identification of the program, directions for using the program, commentary on the functions of various sections of the program, explanation of input or output, etc.

These comments are obtained by use of the **REM** statement whose form is as follows:

REM *comments or remarks*

The **REM** statement may be inserted at any point in the program, and is given a line number. It is not, however, an executable statement, and has no influence on the running of the program. Since the information in the **REM** statement is only printed in the program listing and is otherwise ignored, there are no restrictions on the format of the comments in the **REM** statement. They may extend to the end of the line. If a comment requires more than one line, another **REM** statement is used.

For example, the program in Fig. 2-4 may be identified by the following **REM** statements:

```
5  REM   PROGRAM TO SOLVE FOR THE
6  REM   ROOTS OF A QUADRATIC EQUATION
```

Any number of **REM** statements may be inserted into a program.

2-7. The END Statement

An **END** statement is required in every program, and must be the last statement in the program; that is, it must have the highest line number. For this reason, it is usually convenient to assign it the line number 99999, the highest possible.

2-8. Running BASIC Programs

The procedure for running BASIC programs varies considerably with the specific type of system being used. Most users will be working with terminals consisting either of a teletype or an alphameric cathode ray tube. In a few instances the BASIC program may be punched onto cards and run in a batch mode, with output on a high-speed line printer. Since the use of terminals is more common, we shall restrict our attention to these.

First, a few general comments about entering a BASIC program. Messages to the computer are generally interpreted one line at a time. That is, the user may type the line

```
120   PRINT   R1,R2
```

Up to this point the characters have been transmitted to the computer, but no interpretation has been made by the computer. If the user then depresses the **RETURN** or **NEW LINE** key (depending upon the system), two things happen:

1. The teletype proceeds to the first character on the next line.
2. The BASIC system examines the information contained in the line and determines if it is to take any action.

For statements in the program, some BASIC systems scan the statements for errors as they are entered, while others do not scan until the **RUN** command is entered. We will assume the former for our examples in this section.

Each line in a BASIC program must begin at the left margin with up to five digits with no imbedded blanks or nonnumerical characters. This, of course, constitutes the line number. Following this, blanks are ignored by the BASIC compiler. That is, the line

$$12345 \quad L \quad E \quad TR \quad 1 = (-B + R)/(2 * A)$$

is equivalent to

$$12345 \quad LET \quad R1 = (-B + R)/(2 * A)$$

Of course, the last example is more readable. Furthermore, only one line may be used for each statement, so inserting blanks too freely may not leave enough characters to accommodate the statement.

The first step in running a BASIC program is to get the computer's attention. This usually involves turning on the console, dialing the computer, and entering a valid user code or charge number. On some systems it is also necessary to inform the computer that you want to use BASIC.

There are essentially two types of programs that are run: (1) new programs not yet entered, and (2) old programs that have been entered and saved. Suppose you want to run a new program. Some systems require a name, which may consist of up to six characters on almost all systems and even more on a few. On other systems the program name is required only if you want to save the program to be used at some later time. Most systems will type or display the word **READY** or its equivalent when the computer will accept BASIC statements or other instructions.

For example, the messages encountered during the sign-on procedure for the GE system are as follows (computer printed information is underscored):

<u>USER NUMBER</u>—A123
<u>TYPE OLD OR NEW:</u> NEW
<u>PROBLEM NAME:</u> ROOT
<u>READY</u>

Following the typing of **READY**, the user may enter his BASIC program.

On IBM systems, a typical sign-on procedure is

<u>ON AT 11:30 03/09/70 IMD SJ</u>
<u>USER NUMBER, PASSWORD</u>—ABC123,DEFG12+*
<u>READY</u>

Note that no program name is required.

On some systems, it is necessary to request the BASIC compiler. For example, on the XDS system, following log-in, the computer types a ! symbol, the user types **BA**, and the computer completes the line with **SIC**, giving

<u>!</u> BA<u>SIC</u>

Instead of **READY**, this system uses the "prompt" character > to signal the user that the BASIC system is ready to accept input.

At this point, the computer is ready to accept BASIC statements into a working storage area. This area is updated with each entry from the terminal, and the information in this working area may be displayed on request. It is from this area that the computer compiles and runs BASIC programs.

To illustrate the entry of a new program and the subsequent debugging, consider entering our root solving program as illustrated in Fig. 2-5. On the system

```
>10 READ A,F (CR)
>10 READ A,B,C (CR)
>20 LET R=SQR(B↑2-4*A*C) (CR)
>30 LET R1=(-B+R/(2*A) (CR)

) ILLEGAL  30
>30 LET R1=(= (CR)

= ILLEGAL  30
>30 LET R1=(-B- (CR)

INCOMPLETE  30
>30 LET R1=(-B+R)/(2*A) (CR)
>40 LET R2=(-B-R)/(2*A) (CR)
>50 PRIMT "R1 ="R1,"R2 ="R2 (CR)

>  ILLEGAL   50
>50 PRINT "R1 ="R1,"R2 ="R2 (CR)
>60 DATA 1,3,4 (CR)
>99999 END (CR)
> RUN (CR)
SQRT OF NEG NUMBER  20
R1 =-0.17712   R2 =-2.82288

>LIST (CR)

 MAR 19  9:19

10 READ A,B,C
20 LET R=SQR(B↑2-4*A*C)
30 LET R1=(-B+R)/(2*A)
40 LET R2=(-B-R)/(2*A)
50 PRINT "R1 ="R1,"R2 ="R2
60 DATA 1,3,4
99999 END

> 60 DATA 1,3,2 (CR)
> RUN (CR)
R1 =-1        R2 =-2
```

Fig. 2-5. Entry of a BASIC program.

used for this example, the computer types the "prompt" character > at the beginning of each line. The user then types in whatever it is he wants to enter. He will receive no messages or other response from the computer until he presses the **RETURN** key. This returns the carriage, and signals the computer that the complete message has been entered. Pressing the **RETURN** key does not cause anything to be typed on the output, but for the purposes of this example a character (CR) has been inserted into Fig. 2-5 to indicate points at which the **RETURN** key was depressed.

In Fig. 2-5, the computer typed all lines not beginning with the "prompt" character > .

In entering the first line of the program, we made a keying error, striking **F** instead of **B**. Errors of this type may usually be "erased" by striking the appropriate key (for example, the reverse arrow on the GE system.) That is, on the GE system, the entry

10   READ   A,F←B,C

is equivalent to

10   READ   A,B,C

The reverse arrow causes the preceding character **F** in the above example to be ignored. Alternatively, the entire line may be repeated if desired, as illustrated for line 10 in Fig. 2-5. Whenever a statement is entered with a line number identical to that of a statement previously entered, only the last entry is retained, i.e., all prior entries with that line number are erased.

Upon keying in line 30, we omitted a close parentheses. Immediately after pressing **RETURN,** the computer informs us that we have an illegal statement. We try twice more before finally getting it right. In line 50, we misspelled **"PRINT,"** again obtaining a message from the computer. The computer accepts our last two statements as conforming to the rules of BASIC.

Being satisfied with our entry, we key in **RUN**, which instructs the computer to compile and execute our program. The compiler first reorders the statements according to their line numbers, if necessary, and begins to execute the program. The error message

SQRT OF NEGATIVE NUMBER   20

is typed by the computer followed by values of the two roots. The meaning of this error is that the computer attempted to take the square root of a negative number in line 20. Upon encountering this condition, the computer prints the error message, takes the square root of the absolute value of the argument, and proceeds. Thus answers are generated, but are usually incorrect.

When many errors are made in keying in a program, it sometimes becomes obscure as to exactly what the program actually contains. Insertion of the command **LIST**, as illustrated after the first run in Fig. 2-5, obtains a listing of the current version of the program.

From the data, we see that the computer has been requested to locate the roots of the equation

$$x^2 + 3x + 4 = 0$$

which has complex roots. Since our program was developed for only equations with real roots, this explains the error.

Next, the **DATA** statement is changed to correspond to the equation

$$x^2 + 3x + 2 = 0$$

and the instruction **RUN** is entered again. This time the correct answer is obtained, and the program is assumed to be correct. However, this assumption is not always good, since errors may exist which do not influence the answers for the particular case run. For example, if line 40 had incorrectly read

$$40 \quad R2 \quad = \quad (-B \quad -R)/2*A$$

the same answer would have been obtained.

Since our program now seems to be running correctly, we can proceed with several alternatives:

1. Enter new **DATA** statements to run other cases, entering **RUN** after each new **DATA** statement.
2. Store the program in an area on disk (a computer peripheral device for storing large quantities of information) to be used at a later time. This is accomplished by entering **SAVE** or some similar message on the terminal. The program must have been given a name prior to this so that it may be recalled at some later time.
3. Make subsequent modifications or additions to the program.

Before entering a new program or turning the terminal off, it is necessary to enter **SCRATCH** (or **CLEAR**, depending upon the computer) to erase the program from our working area.

Essentially the same procedure may be followed in running an "old" program that has been "saved" earlier. The first step is to move the program from the storage area into the working area. The procedure for this varies with the system. Once it has been recalled, we proceed as if we had just entered the program from the keyboard.

There are a few other features that should be mentioned. It is possible that the line numbers may no longer follow any logical sequence, or that there may not be sufficient unused line numbers to enter an addition to the program. The computer will automatically renumber the lines in the entire program or subsection thereof by entering the appropriate instructions.

Lines may be deleted entirely by appropriate instructions from the teletype, such as

DEL 80

to delete line 80 on an XDS system. Similar instructions may be used to delete multiple lines or sections of a program. Alternatively, a line may be deleted by typing the line number followed by **RETURN**. On some systems this leaves the line number in the program but without an associated statement, a perfectly acceptable procedure.

Although this situation should not be encountered in the programs for the present chapter, it is quite possible for the computer to execute a program for an excessive period of time, usually indicative of an error in the program logic. The user may terminate a run by inserting the appropriate message, being **STOP** on the GE system. Even if the teletype is printing, depressing the S terminates the output and the remainder of the word may be entered. Other systems use the **ESCAPE** key.

There are a number of other options available from the keyboard. In a manual of this type it is unrealistic to include all types of BASIC systems that are available. Moreover, the operating procedures are changed so frequently that they would be out of date anyway.

2-9. Rounding

Depending upon the computer and depending upon how particular calculations are made by the computer, the student may find that he does not quite get the answers he expects. For example, he may find that

$$1.0+1.0=1.999999$$

The difficulty here is that the computer represents numbers internally in binary notation. Without getting into the details of how this representation is made nor why it is that certain numbers are represented one way while other numbers may be represented in a different manner, let us simply say that the computer cannot exactly represent all the numbers we give it—in fact, it can represent only a few of them. For example, 1.0 would either be represented by **0.9999995** or **1.0000005**, usually the former. Although the error is very small, it can accumulate with lengthy calculations.

Although this phenomenon is bothersome in some cases, it usually only causes certain numbers in the output to appear a bit peculiar, e.g., **4.9999** instead of **5.0000**. This is caused by the computer, and is not any reflection on the BASIC programmer.

2-10. Summary

This chapter has introduced enough of the concepts of BASIC to permit running of several rather simple problems. In the succeeding chapters we shall consider more advanced features of BASIC. Since we will build upon the concepts in this chapter, it is advisable to master the use of the terminal and to run a number of the exercises given below.

Exercises

2-1. Write BASIC expressions to accomplish the following:

†(a) $\dfrac{a + b}{c + d}$

(b) x^3

(c) $a + \dfrac{b}{c + d}$

†(d) $\dfrac{a \cdot b}{c + 10}$

(e) $\dfrac{x + 2}{y + 4}$

(f) $\dfrac{i + j}{k + 3}$

†Solutions to Exercises marked with a dagger (†) are given in Appendix C.

2-2. Write BASIC expressions to accomplish the following:

(a) $\dfrac{i+j}{k+n} + m$

†(b) $\dfrac{a+b}{c+\dfrac{d}{e}}$

(c) $1 + x + \dfrac{x^2}{2!} + \dfrac{x^3}{3!}$ (3! is 3 factorial)

(d) $\dfrac{3 + y + y^2 + 4y^3}{x + 4}$

†(e) $\dfrac{a}{b} + \dfrac{c \cdot d}{e \cdot f \cdot g}$

(f) $\dfrac{1}{x^2}\left(\dfrac{y}{10}\right)^z$

2-3. Write BASIC expressions to accomplish the following:

(a) $2\pi r^2$

(b) $a + x[b + x(c + dx)]$

(c) $\left(\dfrac{a}{b}\right)^{.86c+1}$

†(d) $\left[p\left(\dfrac{r}{s}\right)^{t-1}\right]$

(e) $k^3 + \left(\dfrac{m \cdot n}{2i}\right)^{2k}$

(f) $-\left(\dfrac{-x + y + 27}{z^2}\right)^4$

2-4. Write LET statements to compute the following:

(a) $x = -\dfrac{1}{2a} + \sin(a/2)$

†(b) $x = \cos(y) + x \cdot \sin(z)$

(c) $x = -\sin^3 y$

(d) $x = \cos^{i+2}(y)$

(e) $x = \sqrt{y^3 + 2z^2/6}$

†(f) $x = y \cdot \sin(\pi/z)$

2-5. Write LET statements to compute the following (log denotes $\log_{10}$ and ln denotes $\log_e$):

(a) $x = \dfrac{1 + \cos y}{1 - \cos y}$

†(b) $x = \left|\dfrac{1 + \cos y}{1 - \cos y}\right|$

(c) $x = \log\left|\dfrac{1 + \cos y}{1 - \cos y}\right|$

(d) $x = \pi \cdot \sin^2(y) \cdot \cos^{i+2}(z)$

$\dagger$(e) $x = \log|\tan y|$

(f) $x = y \cdot \log|\arctan(z/3)|$

2-6. Write **LET** statements to compute the following:

(a) $x = \left(\dfrac{10}{\pi yz}\right)^{1/2} \cos y$

$\dagger$(b) $x = (y)^{1/2}(z)^{i+1}(e)^{-y}$

(c) $x = e^{-\sqrt{y/13}}$

(d) $x = \cos\left(e^{-|\sin x|}\right)$

(e) $x = \dfrac{1}{\sqrt{\sin y}} + \left|\dfrac{1}{\sqrt{\cos y}}\right|$

$\dagger$(f) $x = \log\left|\dfrac{1}{\sqrt{\cos y}}\right| \cdot \log|e^{-x}|$

2-7. Prepare a program to read a measurement in feet and print this measurement in centimeters, meters, inches, feet, and yards. The conversion factors are

$$1 \text{ foot} = 12 \text{ inches}$$
$$1 \text{ yard} = 3 \text{ feet}$$
$$1 \text{ inch} = 2.54 \text{ centimeters}$$
$$1 \text{ meter} = 100 \text{ centimeters}$$

The output should appear as follows (for 3 feet):

0.9144	METERS
91.4	CENTIMETERS
36	INCHES
3	FEET
1	YARDS

Run the program for 1.7 feet.

$\dagger$**2-8.** Prepare a program to read a volumetric measurement in cubic feet and convert to gallons (1 cu ft = 7.48 gal), liters (1 cu ft = 28.316 liters), cubic yards (27 cu ft = 1 cu yd), bushels (1 cu ft = 0.8036 bushels), and U.S. liquid barrels (1 bl = 31.5 gal). The output should be analogous to that in the previous exercise. Run the program for 10 cu ft.

2-9. A man borrows P dollars for n years at an interest rate of i. At the end of n years, he owes $P(1 + i)^n$. Write a program that reads P, i (in percent), and n, and calculates the final amount owed. Run for $P = \$100$, $i = 8\%$, and $n = 5$.

2-10. A man borrows a sum of money P. He proposes to repay this amount in n annual installments at an annual interest rate of i. The annual payment is given by

$$M = \frac{Pi\,(1 + i)^n}{(1 + i)^n - 1}$$

The total amount of interest he pays is

$$nM - P$$

Write a BASIC program to compute the annual payment and total interest paid if $5,000 is borrowed at 7% interest for 5 years.

2-11. The sum of the numbers from 1 to n equals $n(n + 1)/2$. Write a program that reads n and calculates the sum. Run the program for $n = 10$.

2-12. Write a program to evaluate the polynomial

$$f(x) = ax^3 + bx^2 + cx + d$$

for given values of a, b, c, d, and x. The number of calculations can be minimized by programming this equation as follows:

$$f(x) = ((ax + b)x + c)x + d$$

Run this program for $a = 1$, $b = 2$, $c = 7$, $d = 4$, and $x = 3$.

2-13. A cubic equation of the form $x^3 + bx^2 + cx + d = 0$ can be reduced to the form $y^3 + py + q = 0$ by the substitution $x = y - b/3$. The equations for p and q are

$$p = (3c - b^2)/3$$

$$q = (27d - 9bc + 2b^3)/27$$

Write a program to compute p and q for $b = 5$, $c = 7$, and $d = 2$. For output print the answer in equation form similar to the following:

$$Y \uparrow 3 + (-1.333)Y + (-0.407)$$

†2-14. An arithmetic progression is a sequence of the type a, $a + d$, $a + 2d, \ldots$, $a + (n - 1)d$ in which each term differs from the preceding term by d, called the *common difference*. The sum of n terms is given by

$$s = \frac{n}{2}[2a + (n - 1)d]$$

Write a BASIC program to compute s for $n = 20$, $a = 1.5$, and $d = 2$.

2-15. A geometric progression is a succession of terms of the type a, ar, $ar^2, \ldots$, ar^{n-1}, where a = first term, r = ratio of successive terms (called the *common ratio*), l = last term, n = number of terms, and s = sum of the terms. Write a BASIC program to compute l and s according to the following equations:

$$l = ar^{n-1}$$

$$s = \frac{a(r^n - 1)}{r - 1}$$

Use $a = 1.5$, $r = .8$, and $n = 20$.

2-16. A combined arithmetic and geometric progression is of the form a, $(a + d)r$, $(a + 2d)r^2, \ldots, [a + (n - 1)d]r^{n-1}$. The sum of n terms is given by

$$s = \frac{a - [a + (n - 1)d]r^n}{1 - r} + \frac{rd(1 - r^{n-1})}{(1 - r)^2}$$

Write a BASIC program to compute s for $a = 1.5$, $d = 2$, $r = 0.8$, and $n = 20$.

Write programs in BASIC to "prove" each of the following trigonometric identities for the specific values of the angle given. Angle is to be entered in degrees, and converted to radians within the program (divide by 57.3 to convert from degrees to radians). Use $x = 30°$, $y = 50°$, $A = 2$, and $B = 1.5$; evaluate each side of the expression; and print the results.

2-17. $\sin(x + y) = \sin x \cos y + \cos x \sin y$

2-18. $\cos(x + y) = \cos x \cos y - \sin x \sin y$

2-19. $\tan(x + y) = \dfrac{\tan x + \tan y}{1 - \tan x \tan y}$

†2-20. $\sin x + \sin y = 2 \sin\left[\dfrac{1}{2}(x + y)\right] \cos\left[\dfrac{1}{2}(x - y)\right]$

2-21. $\sin^2 x - \sin^2 y = \sin(x + y) \sin(x - y)$

2-22. $\cos^2 y - \sin^2 x = \cos(x + y) \cos(x - y)$

2-23. $A \cos x + B \sin x = \sqrt{A^2 + B^2} \sin(x + \alpha): \alpha = \tan^{-1}(A/B)$

2-24. $A \cos x + B \sin x = \sqrt{A^2 + B^2} \cos(\beta - x); \beta = \tan^{-1}(B/A)$

2-25. Consider preparation of a program to compute the area of the shaded region, called a *circular segment*, shown in the figure. It can be computed as follows:

(a) Area of cross-hatched triangle plus circular segment is the area of the circle, πr^2, times the ratio $\theta/2\pi$, or

$$r^2\theta/2$$

(b) The length of the chord, c, is $2r \sin(\theta/2)$.

(c) The height h of the cross-hatched triangle is $r \cos \theta/2$.

(d) The area of the cross-hatched triangle is $hc/2$.

(e) The area of the circular segment is therefore the area of the circular segment plus the cross-hatched triangle computed in part (a) less the area of the triangle computed in part (d).

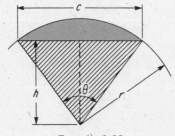

Exercise 2-25.

†2-26. Suppose we construct a parabola as shown in the figure. The length of the parabolic arc is given by

$$\sqrt{4h^2 + b^2} + \frac{b^2}{2h} \ln\left[\frac{2h + \sqrt{4h^2 + b^2}}{b}\right]$$

The area of the section is given by $4bh/3$. Write a BASIC program to compute the area and length of the arc for $h = 6$ and $b = 3$.

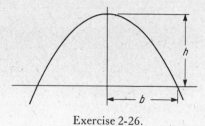

Exercise 2-26.

2-27. Suppose we have a circle of radius r inside of which we want to inscribe a regular polygon with n sides as illustrated in the figure for $n = 4$. The area of this polygon is given by

$$A = \frac{nr^2}{2} \sin\left(\frac{2\pi}{n}\right)$$

The perimeter of the inscribed polygon is given by

$$P = 2nr \sin(\pi/n)$$

Write a BASIC program to compute A and P for $n = 6$ and $r = 4$.

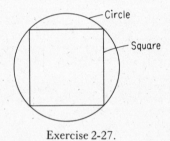

Exercise 2-27.

2-28. The hyperbolic sine and the hyperbolic cosine are given by the equations

$$\sinh x = \frac{e^x - e^{-x}}{2}$$

$$\cosh x = \frac{e^x + e^{-x}}{2}$$

Write a BASIC program to compute these two functions for $x = 2$.

2-29. The complex equations frequently used to give physical properties of materials as functions of other variables can be conveniently solved on the computer. For example, the thermal conductivity of oil shale is given by

$$k_s = 0.57827\,(1.8081 - 0.03698F + 0.00198T + 0.0003056F^2$$

$$- 0.000005184T^2 - 0.00001872FT)$$

where k_s = thermal conductivity, Btu/hr ft² °F/ft
T = temperature, °C
F = oil yield, gal/ton

Prepare a program to compute the thermal conductivity at 45°C of an oil shale whose oil yield is 25 gal/ton.

2-30. The vapor pressure of water between 50°C and 374.11°C is given by the following expression:

$$\log_{10} \frac{p}{p_c} = -\frac{x}{T} \left[\frac{a + bx + cx^3 + ex^4}{1 + dx} \right]$$

where p = vapor pressure, atm

p_c = critical pressure, 218.167 atm

T = temperature in degrees Kelvin = $t(°C) + 273.16$

$x = T_c - T$

T_c = critical temperature, 647.27°K

$a = 3.3463130$

$b = 4.14113 \times 10^{-2}$

$c = 7.515484 \times 10^{-9}$

$d = 1.3794481 \times 10^{-2}$

$e = 6.56444 \times 10^{-11}$

Prepare a program to compute the vapor pressure of water at 75°C.

Chapter 3

TRANSFER OF CONTROL

In the preceding chapter some very simple BASIC programs were illustrated and developed, each of which operated on a more or less "once-through" basis. Programs such as these are encountered quite often, but the more common situation is the one that takes advantage of the very powerful possibilities of logical decision making by the digital computer itself. There are times when the programmer would like to skip certain statements in the program under one set of conditions, or execute those statements under another set of conditions. In other situations the programmer might prefer to go back to the very beginning of the program and read in new sets of data; transfer to the end of the program and terminate its operation; or go to some other intermediate point in the program to begin a new series of calculations. These situations described above give rise to the need for *transfer-of-control* statements, and the purpose of this chapter is to introduce this type of statement and show its usage in BASIC programming.

This aspect of programming makes use of four basic decision-making capabilities of the digital computer. These are:

1. Unconditional transfer of control to the instruction at some prespecified location in the computer's memory other than the next one in sequence. This is commonly called a *branch instruction*.
2. Similar to the previous case except that the transfer occurs only if some number is tested and found to be positive.
3. Similar to the previous case except that transfer occurs only if the number is zero.
4. Similar to the second case except that transfer occurs only if the number is negative.

These capabilities enable the programmer to make logical decisions based on previous calculations and to execute appropriate sections of the program. In addition to branches to alternative sections of the program, he may instruct the computer to repeat a given section of the program a number of times, thereby constructing a loop.

3-1. Flow Charts

With the possibilities for branches and loops within the structure of a computer program, it becomes increasingly more difficult for the programmer to mentally account for all the possible loops and branches. The programs that have been illustrated previously in this book have been relatively simple, but with the introduction of transfer-of-control statements they can be made so complex that it is virtually impossible for the programmer to visualize all of the logical decision loops via a purely mental memory process. Flow charts provide an answer to this problem.

The flow chart is a very simple type of schematic diagram or "road map" which allows the programmer to chart out on paper the logical structure of his computer program. He may indicate all the branches and loops and their interrelationships with one another. The flow chart or block diagram provides a visual representation that not only is helpful to the individual programmer, but it is a valuable part of the documentation of his program and will allow someone else to interpret and use the program with a minimum of difficulty.

Flow charts indicate the "flow of control" between the various statements that comprise the program. The flow chart is normally made up of a set of boxes or shapes which are coded to indicate the nature of the operations involved.

Appendix B at the end of the book gives a complete list of the American Standard flow-chart symbols, but for the purposes of this chapter, the following simple list is sufficient.

A rectangle is used to indicate a processing symbol (typically arithmetic operations).

A diamond is used to indicate a decision and the lines leaving the corners of the diamond are labeled with the decision results that are associated with each path.

The parallelogram is used to indicate any basic input or output symbol. There are, in addition, many special symbols for input-output operations.

An oval is used to indicate either the beginning or the end of a program.

A small circle is used to indicate a connection between two points in a flow chart in situations in which a connecting line between them would clutter the basic flow chart.

Arrows are used to indicate the direction of flow through the flow chart. Every line should have an arrow on it, but the length of the arrow is not important.

Any text or notes may be placed beside or in these symbols. It is especially helpful to indicate numbers beside appropriate processing symbols to indicate the line number that will be associated with that particular operation in the BASIC program.

As our first example, the flow chart of the program in Fig. 1-2 is given in Fig. 3-1. The first step is to read the data, followed by a test to see if the total sales

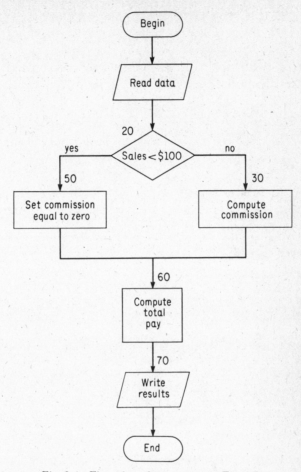

Fig. 3-1. Flow chart for program in Fig. 1-2.

are below $100. If so, statement 50 is executed; if not, statement 30 is executed. In either case, control is eventually transferred to line 60 which computes the total pay. Finally, the results are printed in line 70.

Throughout the remainder of this book are examples of flow charts which should be sufficient to illustrate completely their usage.

It cannot be overemphasized to the beginning programmer that the flow chart represents the first step in the formulation of the program. Many beginning students participate in the very foolish habit of first trying to write their program and *subsequently* constructing a flow chart to illustrate the logic of the program. This is exactly the opposite of the recommended route. It should be noted that beginning programmers cannot always anticipate everything. Often it is not until they have drawn a flow chart and tried to write the BASIC statements that they begin to find flaws in the flow chart.

3-2. The GOTO Statement

In some programs it is necessary to execute the statements in some order other than by their line numbers. One way to alter the normal flow of execution is with the use of the **GOTO** statement, whose format is

$$\textbf{GOTO} \quad \textit{line number}$$

where the *line number* is the line number of another statement.   In Fig. 1-2, a **GOTO** statement is used in line 40 to transfer control directly to line 60, skipping line 50.

```
>LIST

  MAR 19  9:29

10 PRINT "A","B","C","R1","R2"
20 READ A,B,C
30 LET R=SQR(B†2-4*A*C)
40 LET R1=(-B+R)/(2*A)
50 LET R2=(-B-R)/(2*A)
60 PRINT A,B,C,R1,R2
70 GOTO20
80 DATA 1,3,2,1,5,4
99999 END

> RUN
A               B               C           R1          R2
 1              3               2           -1          -2
 1              5               4           -1          -4

OUT OF DATA  20
```

(a) Program

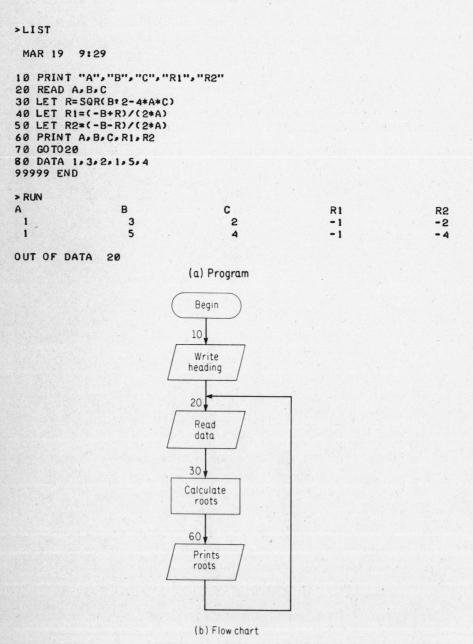

(b) Flow chart

Fig. 3-2. Illustration of use of **GOTO** statement to process more than one set of data.

Another use of the **GOTO** statement is to cause the computer to execute a program for more than one set of data. As an example, consider the modification of our root solving program in Fig. 3-2. The first statement prints the appropriate heading for the output. The program then reads a set of data, calculates the roots, and then prints the answers. The **GOTO** statement then instructs the computer to branch or transfer control to line 20 to read a new set of data and repeat the calculations.

On the first pass through the program the **READ** statement assigns the values 1, 3, and 2 to **A**, **B**, and **C**, respectively. On the second pass, the values 1, 5, and 4 are assigned to **A**, **B**, and **C**. On the third pass, there are no more values remaining in the **DATA** statement to be read. This generates the "**OUT OF DATA**" error message which terminates the program.

Suppose in keying in the program we had mistakenly entered

70   GOTO 30

in the program in Fig. 3-2. Now the read statement is outside of the "loop" generated by the **GOTO** statement. The computer repeatedly cycles through the loop, printing out the roots corresponding to the first set of data. There is nothing in the program to stop the process, which continues until the user keys in a message to stop the process.

Incidentally, it is possible to transfer to a **REM** statement, but this is effectively the same as transferring to the first executable statement following the **REM** statement.

3-3. The IF-THEN Statement

The **GOTO** statement discussed in the preceding section provides a means by which to branch unconditionally to another part of the program. In many cases, this branch is conditional—that is, should be made in certain cases but not in others. For example, suppose we would like to expand our root-solving program to include complex roots as well as real roots. As illustrated by the flow chart in Fig. 3-3, the sign of the expression $b^2 - 4ac$ is used to determine if the roots are real or complex. Then two alternate paths are followed, both terminating with a **GOTO** statement to transfer control back to the **READ** statement to process another set of data.

The decision as to which path the program is to follow is accomplished with the **IF-THEN** statement whose format is

IF *expression relation expression* **THEN** *line number*

The condition between the **IF** and the **THEN** is either "true" or "false." If this condition is "true," control is transferred to the statement whose line number follows the **THEN**. If this condition is "false," control flows as normal to the next statement following the **IF-THEN** statement.

Table 3-1 gives the six conditional operators recognized by the BASIC compiler.

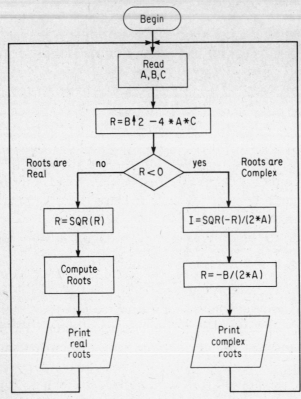

Fig. 3-3. Flow chart for program to solve for
real or imaginary roots.

Figure 3-4 illustrates the use of an **IF-THEN** statement in line 30. If **R** is nega-tive, control is transferred to line 100, which is a **REM** statement. Consequently, the next statement executed is line 110. If **R** is zero or positive, the next statement to be executed is line 50.

TABLE 3-1
Relational Symbols

Symbol	Explanation	Example
$=$	Equal to	IF X$=$Y THEN 30; Control is transferred to line 30 only if X equals Y.
$<>$	Not equal to	IF X$<>$Y THEN 30; Control is transferred to line 30 only if X is not equal to Y.
$<$	Less than	IF X$<$Y THEN 30; Control is transferred to line 30 only if X is less than Y.
$>$	Greater than	IF X$>$Y THEN 30; Control is transferred to line 30 only if X is greater than Y.
$<=$ or $=<$	Less than or equal	IF X$<=$Y THEN 30 or IF X$=<$Y THEN 30; Control is transferred to line 30 only if Y is greater than X.
$>=$ or $=>$	Greater than or equal	IF X$>=$Y THEN 30 or IF X$=>$Y THEN 30; Control is transferred to line 30 only if Y is less than X.

```
>LIST

  MAR 19   9:33

10 READ A,B,C
20 LET R=B↑2-4*A*C
30 IF R<0 THEN 100
40 REM ROOTS ARE REAL
50 LET R=SQR(R)
60 PRINT "ROOTS ARE REAL"
70 PRINT "R1 =" (-B+R)/(2*A),"R2 =" (-B-R)/(2*A)
80 PRINT
90 GOTO10
100 REM ROOTS ARE COMPLEX
110 LET R=SQR(-R)
120 PRINT "ROOTS ARE COMPLEX"
130 PRINT "REAL PART =" -B/(2*A)
140 PRINT "IMAG PART =" R/(2*A)
150 PRINT
160 GOTO10
170 DATA 1,3,2,1,3,4
99999 END

> RUN
ROOTS ARE REAL
R1 =-1              R2 =-2

ROOTS ARE COMPLEX
REAL PART =-1.5
IMAG PART = 1.32288


OUT OF DATA  10
```

Fig. 3-4. Program to determine either real or complex roots.

Although in the **IF-THEN** statement in Fig. 3-4, a variable, **R**, is compared to a constant, zero, an arithmetic expression can be compared to another arithmetic expression. The same results as in Fig. 3-4 could have been obtained by using the statement

$$\text{IF} \quad B{\uparrow}2 < 4*A*C \quad \text{THEN} \quad 100$$

immediately following the **READ** statement. However, this would have necessitated computing **R** in each branch of the program.

In cases in which a set of data is to be entered and then further processing is to be done, the **IF-THEN** statement can be used to detect a "flag" in the input data indicating that all data has been entered. For example, suppose the largest element in a set of data is to be found and printed. Furthermore, suppose the programmer does not know beforehand how many elements are in the set of data, only that there are more than one and that none of them is zero. Then it is possible to let the last number in the **DATA** statements be zero. Upon detecting this zero, the program then terminates the reading of data.

The program in Fig. 3-5 is designed to accomplish the objectives outlined in the previous paragraph. The largest element found so far is stored in **B**. The first statement reads the first element and stores its value in **B**. The next **READ** statement obtains the next element of data. Line 30 checks if its value is zero, transferring to line 70 if so. If **X** is less than **B**, the current element of data is less than

```
LIST

  MAR 25 21:21

10 READ B
20 READ X
30 IF X=0 THEN 70
40 IF X<B THEN 20
50 LET B=X
60 GOTO 20
70 PRINT "LARGEST ELEMENT IS"B
80 DATA 1.7,2.5,-1.2,3.1,4.7,1.9,0
99999 END

> RUN
LARGEST ELEMENT IS 4.7
```

(a) Program

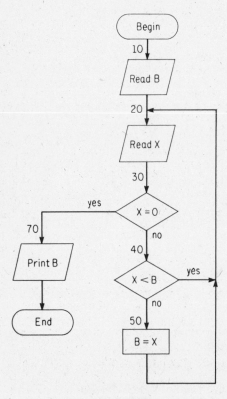

(b) Flow chart

Fig. 3-5.   Use of "end-of-data" to
avoid counting entries.

some previous value, and control is transferred back to the **READ** statement. If not, **B** is assigned the current value of **X**, and control is transferred back to the **READ** statement. The flow chart in Fig. 3-5b illustrates the program logic.

Some recent versions of BASIC permit the words **GOTO** to be used in place of **THEN** in the **IF** statement. For example, line 30 of the program in Fig. 3-5 could be

$$30 \quad IF \quad X=0 \quad GOTO \quad 70$$

Before using this feature, the user should verify that his system recognizes this modification. Since it is not universally accepted, it will not be used in this text.

As another example of a program requiring decisions, consider an oversimplified version of a program that computes the service charge on a bank account. Suppose we insert the balance at the beginning of the month as the first entry in a **DATA** statement. Subsequent entries correspond to deposits or checks, the latter being indicated by a negative entry. These are in the same order as processed by the bank during the month. The end of transactions is indicated by a zero entry. The service charge is computed as 50¢ plus 4¢ per check on all checks over 5, less 10¢ per each $100 in the minimum balance. No service charge is made on accounts for which the minimum balance exceeds $400. Subtract service charge to obtain final balance. Print final balance and service charge.

The flow chart and program for this exercise are shown in Fig. 3-6. This program must compute the current balance, determine the minimum balance, count the number of checks, and compute the service charge. Notice that the program contains five **IF-THEN** statements:

1. In line 60 to determine if transaction is zero.
2. In line 90 to determine if current balance is less than previous minimum.
3. In line 120 to determine if transaction was a check.
4. In line 160 to determine if minimum balance exceeded $400.
5. In line 190 to determine if there were more than five checks.

Each of these serves a specific purpose, and the relationship between all of these is best given by the flow chart in Fig. 3-6a.

3-4. Debugging

In previous programs, bugs could be located rather easily by tracing back through the program statement by statement. But now that the program contains statements that make decisions, this can no longer be done so readily. Instead, it is much easier to insert a few print statements to display some intermediate results to assist in debugging.

To illustrate this procedure, suppose we insert an intentional "bug" in line 90 of the program in Fig. 3-6b; namely, transferring to line 110 if $M > B$ instead of when $M < B$. This gives erroneous results for the first run in Fig. 3-7. One cannot always uncover bugs of this type by inspecting the program, although this is logically the first step.

If this is unsuccessful, the next step is to insert a print statement to display intermediate results. Suppose we insert a statement following the read statement in line 50 to print the current balance, the minimum balance, the number of checks already processed, and the transaction that is about to be processed. From the output in Fig. 3-7, we note that we have found the maximum balance rather than the minimum balance, which leads us almost directly to line 90 to look for the error. The output also verifies that our program is counting the number of checks correctly.

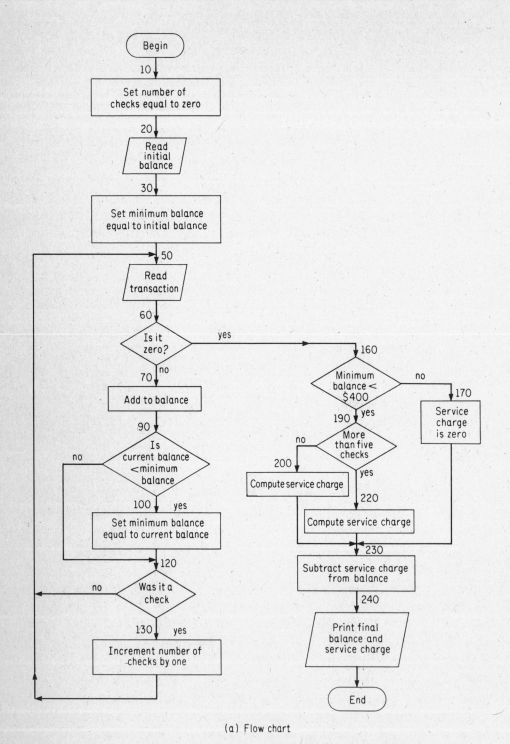

(a) Flow chart

Fig. 3-6. Program for computing service charge on bank accounts.

```
LIST

JUL 31 12:33

10 LET N=0
20 READ B
30 LET M=B
40 REM READ A TRANSACTION
50 READ T
60 IF T=0 THEN 160
70 LET B=B+T
80 REM UPDATE MINIMUM BALANCE
90 IF M<B THEN 110
100 LET M=B
110 REM UPDATE NUMBER OF CHECKS
120 IF T>0 THEN 50
130 LET N=N+1
140 GOTO 50
150 REM COMPUTE SERVICE CHARGE
160 IF M<400 THEN 190
170 LET S=0
180 GOTO 230
190 IF N>5 THEN220
200 LET S=.5-.001*M
210 GOTO 230
220 LET S = .5 +.04*(N-5)-.001*M
230 LET B=B-S
240 PRINT "BALANCE" B,"SERVICE CHARGE" S
250 DATA 370.14,88.21,-22.84,-19.72,-26.14,-27.04,48.00
260 DATA -97.26,-18.49,-106.22,172.49,0
99999 END




>RUN
BALANCE 360.739                    SERVICE CHARGE 0.39136

>
```

(b) Program

Fig. 3-6 (continued).

Correcting this "bug" and deleting the **PRINT** statement gives the desired results from our program.

3-5. Counters

One use of an **IF-THEN** statement is to construct a counter. Suppose we have 5 data points for which we want to compute the arithmetic average. One way to accomplish this would be as follows:

```
10 READ D1,D2,D3,D4,D5
20 LET S=D1+D2+D3+D4+D5
30 LET A=S/5
40 PRINT A
50 DATA 1,7,2,-1,5
99999 END
```

```
LIST

   JUL 31 12:40

   10 LET N=0
   20 READ B
   30 LET M=B
   40 REM READ A TRANSACTION
   50 READ T
   60 IF T=0 THEN 160
   70 LET B=B+T
   80 REM UPDATE MINIMUM BALANCE
   90 IF M>B THEN 110
   100 LET M=B
   110 REM UPDATE NUMBER OF CHECKS
   120 IF T>0 THEN 50
   130 LET N=N+1
   140 GOTO 50
   150 REM COMPUTE SERVICE CHARGE
   160 IF M<400 THEN 190
   170 LET S=0
   180 GOTO 230
   190 IF N>5 THEN220
   200 LET S=.5-.001*M
   210 GOTO 230
   220 LET S = .5 +.04*(N-5)-.001*M
   230 LET B=B-S
   240 PRINT "BALANCE" B,"SERVICE CHARGE" S
   250 DATA 370.14,88.21,-22.84,-19.72,-26.14,-27.04,48.00
   260 DATA -97.26,-18.49,-106.22,172.49,0
   99999 END

>RUN
BALANCE 361.13                    SERVICE CHARGE 0

>55 PRINT B,M,N,T
>RUN
   370.14          370.14          0          88.21
   458.35          458.35          0         -22.84
   435.51          458.35          1         -19.72
   415.79          458.35          2         -26.14
   389.65          458.35          3         -27.04
   362.61          458.35          4          48
   410.61          458.35          4         -97.26
   313.35          458.35          5         -18.49
   294.86          458.35          6         -106.22
   188.64          458.35          7          172.49
   361.13          458.35          7          0
BALANCE 361.13                    SERVICE CHARGE 0

>90 IF M<B THEN 110
>55
>RUN
BALANCE 360.739                   SERVICE CHARGE 0.39136
```

Fig. 3-7. Illustration of the use of PRINT statements as a debugging aid.

Even for this small number, the program is cumbersome. What if you had a hundred data points? For all practical purposes, it would be impossible to accomplish it in this manner.

Suppose we proceed as follows. First, initialize the sum S to zero. Then read one data point and add to the old value of S to obtain the new value of S. After doing this five times (this is where the counter enters the picture), we have the sum of all the data points. From here on we can proceed as before.

Consider the following statements to accomplish our task:

```
10 LET S=0
20 LET J=0
30 LET J=J+1
40 READ D
50 LET S=S+D
60 IF J<5 THEN 30
70 LET A=S/5
80 PRINT A
90 DATA 1,7,2,-1,5
99999 END
```

The counter is composed of the following statements:

```
20   LET   J=0
30   LET   J=J+1
60   IF   J<5   THEN   30
```

The purpose of line 20 is to initialize our counter, J, to zero. Line 30 increments J by 1 on each pass, indicating that another number is being processed. Line 60 checks to see if our count has reached its ultimate value. It is the statements between lines 30 and 60 that are repeated five times.

Of course, it is possible to construct counters that are incremented by steps other than one by simply changing line 30 of the above example.

The advantage of using the counter for our problem is that the complexity of the program is independent of the number of data points. That is, by modifying line 60 to read

```
IF   J<100   GOTO   30
```

and line 70 to read

```
LET   A=S/100
```

our program can handle a hundred data points just as easily as it could handle five. Alternatively, we could assign a variable N equal to 100 and use N in lines 60 and 70.

3-6. The ON-GOTO Statement

Although the unconditional GOTO and the IF-THEN statements are the most commonly used statements for altering the normal execution sequence, the ON-GOTO can in some instances replace several IF-THEN statements. The format of this statement is

ON *expression* GOTO *line number, line number, etc.*

The processing of this statement proceeds as follows:

1. The expression is evaluated.
2. The integer part of the expression is evaluated, that is, INT(*expression*).

Recall that fractional parts are truncated, so that rounding, if desired, must be included in the expression.

3. If the result is 1, control is transferred to the first line number; if the result is 2, control is transferred to the second line number; etc.

4. If the result is less than one or if the result is greater than the ordinal position of the last line number, an error message is generated.

There is no limit on the number of line numbers that may be used; however, they must all fit on one line.

As an example, suppose we are to process data on students in a class. Let one item of our data be the student's classification, 1 standing for freshman, 2 for sophomore, etc. If the variable C represents the student's classification, the statement

$$90 \quad \text{ON} \quad \text{C} \quad \text{GOTO} \quad 210, \quad 330, \quad 460, \quad 570$$

transfers control to line number 210 if C equals 1, to line number 330 if C equals 2, to line 460 if C equals 3, and to line 570 if C equals 4. If C is less than 1 or greater than 4, an error message is generated.

3-7. The STOP Statement

In many cases, one branch of an IF-THEN statement logically leads to the termination of the program. There are two avenues to terminate execution of the program. The first of these is to transfer to the END statement, for example,

$$70 \quad \text{GOTO} \quad 99999$$

where line 99999 is

$$99999 \quad \text{END}$$

The second alternative is to use the STOP statement, which is simply

$$70 \quad \text{STOP}$$

The results of either of these is the same—the execution of the program is terminated.

3-8. In Summary

The transfer of control statements, especially the GOTO and the IF-THEN statements, are a very useful feature of BASIC. These statements form a very important part of all programs of any complexity. The examples presented below require their use. In these exercises, a counter for the number of data entries should be constructed only when absolutely necessary or is so requested in the problem. That is, it is permissible to simply terminate the program with an "end of data" message whenever the objectives of the problem can be met in this manner.

Exercises

Modify the following exercises to accept more than one set of data:

3-1. Exercise 2-10.

3-2. Exercise 2-12.

3-3. Exercise 2-16.

3-4. Exercise 2-26.

†3-5. A purchaser buys x units of a product that normally costs $1.75 a unit. However, on all units purchased over and above 100, he gets a 10% discount. Furthermore, on all units purchased above 300, he gets a 30% discount from the base price of $1.75 a unit. Prepare a program that obtains the purchaser number and the number of units he buys from a **DATA** statement, and prints the purchaser number and the amount of his bill in columnar fashion with suitable headings. Use as data

Purchaser Number	Units Purchased
177	75
201	398
141	147
102	181

The program should repeat the calculation until all entries in the **DATA** statements are processed.

3-6. Consider a program to compute the coins to be given in change for the following situation:

(a) All purchases are under $1.00.

(b) Purchaser will always present a dollar bill.

(c) Change should consist of the minimum number of coins.

(d) Only pennies, nickels, dimes, and quarters will be given in change.

The program obtains the amount of the purchase from a **DATA** statement. The program should be written to run more than one case. Output should be in columns with amount of purchase, number of pennies, number of nickels, etc., with appropriate headings. Run the program for purchases of 97¢, 78¢, 54¢, 21¢, and 1¢. This program can be prepared using the **INT** function and no **IF-THEN** statements, or by using **IF-THEN** statements and not using the **INT** function. Try both ways.

3-7. Consider a program to compute the flight time for a sequence of airplane flights. The data on each flight consist of the flight number, the departure time, and the arrival time. The times will be entered on the 24-hour system, i.e., 8:10 p.m. would be entered as 2010. Note that the last two digits in this system never exceed 60. It is also known that no flight lasts over 24 hours, so a flight with a departure time of 2300 and an arrival time of 0115 takes 2 hours and 15 minutes. The program's output should be as follows:

Flight	Hours	Minutes
809	2	15
911	4	20

Use the following as input data:

Flight No.	Departure Time	Arrival Time
817	0915	1245
122	0945	1215
405	2140	0020
101	1710	1850

3-8. Wheeler Dealer is the leading automobile dealer in the state. He now spends $2,000 a month on advertising, and sells 200 cars a month at about $300 profit per car. From this, he must subtract another $10,000 as fixed operating costs which are independent of the volume of sales. An advertising agency tells Wheeler that each time he doubles the amount he spends on advertising, he will increase the volume of sales by 20%. Write a program that gives Wheeler the amount spent on advertising, the number of sales he makes, and his net profit. Begin with his current status and successively double the amount of advertising until his net profit "goes over the hump," i.e., begins to decline. The output should appear as follows:

Advertising	Units Sold	Net Profit
2000	200	48000
4000	240	58000
8000	288	68400
16000	346	77800
32000	415	82500
64000	498	75400

3-9. Prepare a program that reads the date in the form of three two-digit numbers (e.g., 02, 19, 67) and prints the date in a form such as **FEBRUARY 19, 1967.** If the month is greater than 12 or if the day is greater than 31, print the words **ERRONEOUS DATE.**

3-10. Write a program to condense some statistics on the students in a class. One set of data is provided for each student, and contains (1) his or her age; (2) the student's sex, the code being 1–male, 2–female; and (3) the student's standing, the code being 1–freshman, 2–sophomore, 3–junior, 4–senior. The output should be the average age of the students, the percent males, and the percent freshmen, sophomore, juniors, and seniors. The number of entries are not counted, so use a zero set of entries to indicate the end of the data. Use the following data:

19	1	1
24	1	4
20	2	2
21	1	2
18	2	1
27	1	4

20	1	2
21	2	3
21	2	2
20	1	2

3-11. Suppose three temperatures, T1, T2, and T3, are entered into a program via a DATA statement. These temperatures may be in any order, but the program is to print them in ascending order, i.e., smallest first, largest last. Using IF-THEN statements, prepare a program to accomplish this objective. Use as data 190, 271, and 147 for T1, T2, and T3 respectively.

†3-12. A man borrows $200 at an interest rate of 1 1/2% per month. He proposes to repay this at the rate of $10 per month. How many full payments must he make, and what must be paid in the final month to leave a balance of exactly zero? Program this problem. The calculations for each month should be as follows:

(a) Calculate the interest for that month, which is 1 1/2% of the current balance.

(b) Add the interest to the current balance to obtain the total amount owed at the end of the month (before receipt of payment).

(c) Subtract the payment to obtain the new balance. For the first month, the interest is $(1\ 1/2\%) \cdot (\$200) = \$3$. The new balance is $\$200 + \$3 - \$10 = \$193$.

3-13. A man plans to invest $500 per year at 6% interest. How many years will be required to accumulate $10,000? Write a BASIC program to compute this. Print the number of years along with the total value of his investments when they first exceed $10,000. The calculations proceed as follows. After the first year, the value of the investment is $\$500 \cdot (1 + 0.06) = \$530$. After the second year, the value is $(\$500 + \$530) \cdot (1 + 0.06) = \$1,091.30$.

†3-14. Consider writing a program that would compute the arithmetic average of the absolute values of a set of data. However, suppose that it is undesirable to count the number of values in this set of data. If it is known beforehand that none of the values will be exactly zero, the computer can be programmed to read succesive values until a value of zero is detected as discussed in Sec. 3-3. Write a program that computes the arithmetic average of the values 0.7, 1.9, −2.2, 7.1, 17.0, −4.2, 7.9, and −5.1. The program should print and appropriately label the total number of values and the arithmetic average.

3-15. Write a program similar to the one in the previous exercise except that the geometric mean of the absolute values is computed. The geometric mean of n values is the nth root of their product.

3-16. The area bounded by the inequalities

$$y < 3$$
$$x + y > 1$$
$$y < 2x + 1$$
$$y > x^2$$

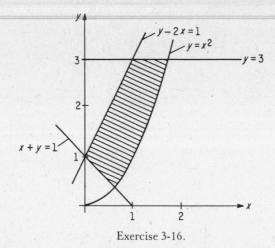

Exercise 3-16.

is illustrated in the associated figure. Write a program that accepts the coordinates of a point and determines if it is within the shaded area. The computer output should be either **YES** or **NO**.

3-17. Prepare a program to read an integer number and determine if it is even. This can be done by dividing by 2 and checking to see if the result is an integer. If the number is even, print the number followed by **IS EVEN**. Do likewise if the number is odd. Run the program for -5, -24, 17, and 8. What would this program tell us about zero?

†3-18. To seven decimal places, the fraction 1/7 is given as 0.1428571. Suppose you wanted it expressed to twenty decimal places. Can you devise a procedure to calculate the digits one by one and prepare a program utilizing it?

3-19. One of the following inequalities is incorrect:

$$|a + b| \leq |a| + |b|$$

$$|a + b| \geq |a| - |b|$$

$$|a - b| \geq |a| + |b|$$

$$|a + b| \leq |a| - |b|$$

Write a program that reads a value for a, a value for b, and checks these four inequalities. The program should print the incorrect inequality as it would be programmed in BASIC. Running the program for the following values of a and b should check all possibilities:

a	b
1	1
1	-1
-1	-1
-1	1

3-20. One method of finding the square root is to use the iterative formula

$$S_{i+1} = \frac{1}{2}\left(\frac{X}{S_i} + S_i\right)$$

where S_i is the estimate of X on the ith iteration. For $X = 300$ and starting with $S = 15$, continue to iterate until the value of S does not change in the fourth decimal place between successive iterations. As output, print the results of this procedure along with the results using the **SQR** function. What changes would you make in the program to compute the square root of 10,000,000? Of 0.001? (*Hint*: One way to make the test for changes in the fourth decimal is to express the equation in the form

$$S_{i+1} = S_i + \frac{1}{2}\left(\frac{x}{S_i} - S_i\right)$$

Now when $\frac{1}{2}\left|\frac{x}{S_i} - S_i\right|$ is less than 0.0001, the solution is found according to our criterion.)

3-21. Another way to formulate the method in the above exercise is as follows. To calculate the square root of a number, say b, select any number, say g_1, and compute another number, say h_1, as follows:

$$h_1 = \frac{b}{g_1}$$

The next step is to average g_1 and h_1 to obtain g_2:

$$g_2 = \frac{g_1 + h_1}{2}$$

Then h_2 is computed as before:

$$h_2 = \frac{b}{g_2}$$

This procedure can be generalized as follows:

$$h_i = \frac{b}{g_i}$$

$$g_{i+1} = \frac{g_i + h_i}{2}$$

The sequences $g_1, g_2, \ldots, g_i$ and $h_1, h_2, \ldots, h_i$ both approach the square root of b. The stopping criterion is whenever

$$|g_i - h_i| < \epsilon$$

where ϵ is a small but positive number. Use this program to take the square roots of 4 and 2, starting with $g_1 = 1$ in both cases and using $\epsilon = 0.00001$.

3-22. The cube root S of a number X can be calculated using the iteration formula

$$S_{i+1} = \frac{2}{3}S_i + \frac{X}{3S_i^2}$$

The iterative procedure may be initialized by setting $S_1 = 1$. Write a computer program to take cube roots of numbers in this manner. For informative purposes, print the value of S after each iteration. Terminate the procedure when the change in S from one iteration to the next is less than 0.01% of the current value of S. The above formula will work for positive or negative values of X, so your program should work likewise. Run the program for $X = 235$ and $X = -91.6$.

†**3-23.** Let the function $F(X)$ be defined as $(X + 2)/(X + 1)$. Define the sequence

$$a_i = F(a_{i-1})$$

Write a computer program to compute the first ten terms of the sequence. What does it converge to?

3-24. The two sequences

$$a_i = \sqrt{a_{i-1} b_{i-1}}$$

$$b_i = \frac{a_{i-1} + b_{i-1}}{2}$$

$$a_1 = a, \quad b_1 = b, \quad a \le b$$

converge to the same limit, called the "arithmetic-geometric mean." Write a program that reads a and b, checks to be sure that $a \le b$ (if not, interchange a and b), and computes the sequence until $|a_i - b_i| < \epsilon$. Run the program for $a = 2$, $b = 7$, and $\epsilon = 0.00001$.

3-25. The Fibonacci numbers, 1, 1, 2, 3, 5, 8, 13, etc., are computed by the following recurrence relationship:

$$a_i = a_{i-1} + a_{i-2}$$
$$a_1 = 1$$
$$a_2 = 1$$

Write a program to compute the first twenty Fibonacci numbers. Also compute the ratio a_i/a_{i-1}, and print alongside the Fibonacci numbers. As the ratio should approach $1 + \sqrt{5}/2$ as more and more terms are calculated, print this value alongside the ratio so that they may be readily compared.

3-26. One of the problems with the computer's **ATN(X)** routine is that it places the result in the first quadrant if $X > 0$ and in the fourth quadrant if $X < 0$. However, if the arctangent of the ratio A/B is to be taken, then depending upon the signs of A and B, the result can be placed in the proper quadrant as illustrated in the accompanying figure. Write a program that reads **A** and **B**, computes the arctangent, places the result in the proper quadrant, converts the result to degrees (between $-180°$ and $+180°$), and prints **A**, **B**, and the angle. Run the program for the following values:

A	B
2	1
-1	2
1	2
-2	-1

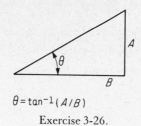

$$\theta = \tan^{-1}(A/B)$$

Exercise 3-26.

Quadrant II	Quadrant I
$A > 0$	$A > 0$
$B < 0$	$B > 0$
$90° < \theta < 180°$	$0 < \theta < 90°$
Quadrant III	Quadrant IV
$A < 0$	$A < 0$
$B < 0$	$B > 0$
$-180° < \theta < -90°$	$-90° < \theta < 0$

3-27. The function e^x can be represented by the infinite series

$$e^x = 1 + x + \frac{x^2}{2} + \frac{x^3}{6} + \frac{x^4}{24} + \cdots$$

Note that the nth term is simply the previous term multiplied by $x/(n-1)$. Compute e^x using this series, stopping when the magnitude of the term being added is less than 10^{-6}. Run the program for $x = 1.7$ and $x = 1.8$. Print the answers in the form

$$\text{EXP} \quad (0.25) = 0.780$$

3-28. Suppose we want to fire a missile at an aircraft when it is directly overhead as illustrated in the figure. To do this, we must know the altitude h of the

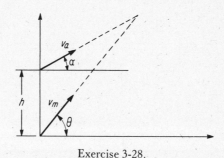

Exercise 3-28.

plane, its velocity v_a, and its angle α with the horizontal. The angle at which to fire the missile is

$$\theta = \cos^{-1}\left[\frac{v_a \cos \alpha}{v_m}\right]$$

where v_m is the velocity of the missile. If the ratio $v_a \cos \alpha / v_m$ is greater than one, the arc cosine does not exist, which means that the aircraft is too fast for us to intercept. Furthermore, we can only aim at angles between 20° and 70°. The intercept time t_e is

$$t_e = \frac{h}{v_m \sin \theta - v_a \sin \alpha}$$

If t_e exceeds 10 sec, our missile fuel is expended and we cannot intercept.

Write a program that, from values of v_a, h, α, and v_m entered via a **DATA** statement, computes whether we should fire the missile. If we can make a hit, the computer should print **FIRE AT ANGLE** and give the angle in degrees; if not, it should print **DO NOT FIRE—CANNOT INTERCEPT**.

Let the velocity of the missile be 1,800 ft/sec. Run the following cases

v_a	α	h
2,000	0°	1,000
600	30°	1,400
1,200	30°	5,000

Note: $\cos^{-1} x = \tan^{-1} (\sqrt{1 - x^2}/x)$

3-29. Suppose we are given an angle and two sides of a triangle. Specifically, suppose a, b, and θ in the accompanying figure are given, and we are to find the third side c. For this problem, there may be no solution, one solution, or two solutions. These can be determined as follows:

1. The angle θ and side a can be used to form a right triangle, and the sides h and y can be calculated from

$$h = a \sin \theta$$
$$y = a \cos \theta$$

2. If b is less than h, no solution exists.
3. If b equals h, only one solution exists, namely, the right triangle. The third side therefore equals y.
4. If b is greater than h, the length x is computed from

$$x = \sqrt{b^2 - h^2}$$

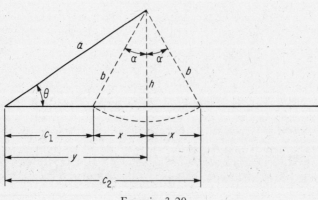

Exercise 3-29.

Two further possibilities exist:

(a) If x is less than y, then two solutions exist, namely, $y + x$ and $y - x$.

(b) If x is greater than y, then only one solution exists,—namely, $y + x$.

Write a program to compute the number of solutions and print the results in the following fashion.

ANGLE	SIDE	SIDE	THIRD SIDE	
30	2	0.5	NO SOLUTION	
30	2	1.5	2.85	0.61
30	2	3.0	4.56	

Run the program for the following cases:

a	b	θ
2	0.5	30°
2	1.5	30°
2	3.0	30°

†3-30. The solution of the simultaneous equations

$$a_1 x + b_1 y = c_1$$
$$a_2 x + b_2 y = c_2$$

is known to be

$$x = \frac{c_1 b_2 - c_2 b_1}{b_2 a_1 - b_1 a_2}$$

$$y = \frac{a_1 c_2 - a_2 c_1}{b_2 a_1 - b_1 a_2}$$

if $b_2 a_1 - b_1 a_2 \neq 0$. Write a program that computes x and y and prints the solution as shown in the figure. If there is no solution, the program should write **NO SOLUTION**. Enter the coefficients via a **DATA** statement. Run the program for the equations

$$3x - 2y = 4$$
$$x + y = 7$$

3-31. In Exercise 2-30, an equation was given for the vapor pressure of water from 50°C to 374.11°C. From 10°C to 150°C, the recommended equation is:

$$\log_{10} \frac{p}{p_c} = -\frac{x}{T} \left[\frac{a' + b'x + c'x^3}{1 + d'x} \right]$$

where $a' = 3.2437814$

$b' = 5.86826 \times 10^{-3}$

$c' = 1.1702379 \times 10^{-8}$

$d' = 2.1878462 \times 10^{-3}$

Other parameters are as defined in Exercise 2-30. Prepare a program to compute the vapor pressure of water using the above equation for temperatures below 100°C and the equation in Exercise 2-30 for temperatures above 100°C. Run the program for temperatures of 45°C, 90°C, and 120°C.

3-32. The reaction rate constant for the decomposition of kerogen is given by the following equations:

$$\log_{10} k = -13572/T + 18.45, \qquad T < 710°K$$
$$\log_{10} k = -5549/T + 7.14, \qquad T \geq 710°K$$

where k = reaction rate constant, min^{-1}

T = temperature, degrees Kelvin

Prepare a program to compute the reaction rate constant at temperatures of 640°K, 720°K, and 810°K.

Chapter 4

LOOPS

In the previous chapter we used **GOTO** and **IF-THEN** statements to cause certain statements in a program to be executed repeatedly. We also introduced a counter via which we could execute certain statements a desired number of times. This chapter introduces the use of the **FOR-NEXT** pair of statements to facilitate the construction of certain types of loops within a program.

4-1. The FOR and NEXT Statements

Suppose we want to compute the sum of all integer numbers from 1 to 100, that is, $\sum_{i=1}^{100} i$. Using the counter discussed in Sec. 3-4 to accomplish this objective, the resulting section of the program would be

```
100 LET S=0
110 LET I=1
120 LET S=S+I
130 LET I=I+1
140 IF I<=100 THEN 120
```

We have effectively created a loop with the counter, since statement 120 is repeated a hundred times.

The use of **FOR** and **NEXT** statements can greatly simplify this procedure, although the effective results are identical. The general format of the **FOR** statement is

FOR *variable* = *expression* **TO** *expression* **STEP** *expression*

This statement is used in conjunction with the **NEXT** statement, whose general format is

NEXT *variable*

The **FOR-NEXT** statements form a *pair*, and neither can be used alone. The **FOR** statement is at the beginning or head of the loop; the **NEXT** statement appears at the foot or end of the loop.

For example, the sum of the integer numbers from 1 to 100 can be obtained with the statements

```
100 LET S=0
110 FØR I=1 TØ 100 STEP 1
120 LET S=S+I
130 NEXT I
```

Note that the variable immediately following **FOR** in line 110 is identical to the variable following **NEXT** in line 130. It is according to this variable that the pairing of **NEXT** and **FOR** statements is made. Using only **NEXT** or, for example, **NEXT L** (variable does not match variable in **FOR** statement) would generate an error message.

In executing the statements in the above segment of the program, the first time the **FOR** statement is encountered, the variable I (often called the *index* of the loop) is assigned the value of 1. Statement 120 is then executed. Upon encounter of the **NEXT** statement, the value of I is increased by 1. If the result is less than or equal to 100, line 120 (the statement following the **FOR** statement) is executed again. If I is greater than 100, the statement following the **NEXT** statement is executed. It should be noted that the procedure is the same as that of the counter presented at the beginning of this section.

As another example, suppose we want to compute the square roots of the integers from A through B, which will be integers obtained via a **READ** statement. Figure 4-1 gives the program to accomplish this along with the output for a typical case. The execution of the program proceeds as shown below:

Line	Result
10	Prints headings
20	Assigns 2 to **A**; 4 to **B**
30	Sets **X** = 2
40	Prints 2, $\sqrt{2}$
50	Sets **X** = 3; return to line 40
40	Prints 3, $\sqrt{3}$
50	Sets **X** = 4, return to line 40
40	Prints 4, $\sqrt{4}$
50	Sets **X** = 5; exceeds value of **B**; sets **X** = 4; proceeds to statement following line 50
60	Nonexecutable statement
70	End

The flow chart for this program is also shown in Fig. 4-1. The flow chart is constructed around the logic involved in the **FOR** and **NEXT** statements rather than incorporating the statements directly.

Whenever the variable in the **FOR** statement is to be incremented by 1, the **STEP** portion of the **FOR** statement may be omitted. That is, the statement

$$\textbf{FOR} \quad \textbf{X} = \textbf{A} \quad \textbf{TO} \quad \textbf{B}$$

implies that **X** is to be incremented by 1 upon encounter of the **NEXT** statement.

A few further comments are in order regarding the expressions in the **FOR** statement. Recall that its general form is

$$\textbf{FOR } variable = expr_1 \textbf{ TO } expr_2 \textbf{ STEP } expr_3$$

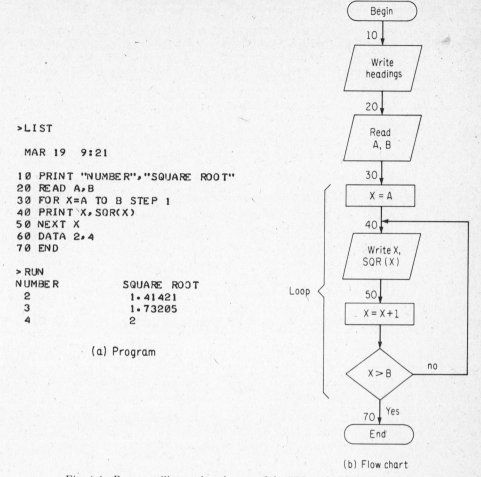

```
>LIST

  MAR 19  9:21

10 PRINT "NUMBER","SQUARE ROOT"
20 READ A,B
30 FOR X=A TO B STEP 1
40 PRINT X,SQR(X)
50 NEXT X
60 DATA 2,4
70 END

> RUN
NUMBER              SQUARE ROOT
   2                   1.41421
   3                   1.73205
   4                   2
```

(a) Program

(b) Flow chart

Fig. 4-1. Program illustrating the use of the **FOR** and **NEXT** statements.

where *expr* stands for expression.   Upon initial encounter of the **FOR** statement, $expr_1$ is evaluated and the result assigned to the *variable* (or index) in the **FOR** statement.   Upon encounter of the **NEXT** statement, $expr_3$ is evaluated and its result added to the current value of the *variable*.   Then $expr_2$ is evaluated, and if the result exceeds the current value of *variable*, the statements in the loop are repeated starting with the first statement following the **FOR** statement.   Upon successive encounters of the **NEXT** statement, the same computations are made as upon the first encounter.   The net result is that $expr_1$ is evaluated only once, but $expr_2$ and $expr_3$ are evaluated as many times as the loop is repeated.   This permits these expressions to contain values that may change during execution of the statements in the loop.   However, if their values are known *not* to change, then it would be more efficient to precompute the values of these expressions in **LET** statements prior to the **FOR** statement, store the results in variables, and use the variables in the **FOR** statement instead of the expressions.

That is, suppose the values of **A** and **B** do not change.   The statement

```
FOR X=SQR(A) TO 2*(A+SQR(B)) STEP B+1
```

would be more efficiently programmed as

```
LET E2=2*(A+SQR(B))
LET E3=B+1
FOR X=SQR(A) TO E2 STEP E3
```

There is no incentive to precompute SQR(A), since this expression is evaluated only once anyway.

It should be noted that the statements in the loop are executed at least once. Execution of the FOR statement essentially only assigns a value, namely that of $expr_1$, to the index. The statements in the loop are executed, and then the index is compared to $expr_2$ at the NEXT statement.

The statements in the loop may contain GOTO statements which may transfer control to statements either inside the loop or outside the loop. A GOTO statement outside the loop may transfer control to a statement inside the loop provided the value of the variable inside the FOR statement is initialized properly.

To illustrate these concepts further, consider preparation of a program to compute the factors of a number. The procedure will be to obtain the number from a DATA statement, and then try division by successive integers, starting with 2, until we know no other factors exist. That is, suppose we consider finding the factors of 420, which incidentally factors into $2 \times 2 \times 3 \times 5 \times 7 = 420$. We begin by dividing 420 by 2, and seeing if the result is an integer. Since $420/2 = 210$, 2 is a factor. However, since there may be multiple factors, we try 2 again. Since $210/2 = 105$, 2 is a repeated factor. Trying 2 again gives $105/2 = 52.5$, which is not an integer. Therefore, we try 3, giving $105/3 = 35$, and 3 is a factor. We try 3 again, obtaining $35/3 = 11.67$. Since this is not an integer, we proceed to 4, and so forth. We can stop searching when we obtain a result of 1 after dividing by a prospective factor.

Figure 4-2 gives the program, the output for a typical run, and the flow chart for this program. Note the two IF-THEN statements within the loop, one of which transfers to a statement outside the loop. Also, note the absence of the STEP specification in the FOR statement, thus implying an increment of 1. Finally, note that the IF-THEN statement in line 50 transfers control to the NEXT statement, thus signifying the completion of one iteration of the loop. A common mistake made by beginning programmers is to transfer control to the FOR statement in these situations. However, this causes the computer to initiate processing of the loop from the very start (i.e., X=2), which is not the desired result.

If one really wanted to write an efficient factoring program, several improvements in the program in Fig. 4-2 could be made. One simple improvement would be to note that the index need be incremented only up to SQR(A). That is, if A/I equals J for I > J, we would have previously found the root when I assumed the value of J. Further improvement could be obtained if the index were incremented up to SQR(A1). The final value of the index is now being changed dynamically as the loop executes.

Another modification is made by noting that after all factors of 2 are removed, only odd numbers need to be checked by the loop. Programming in this manner

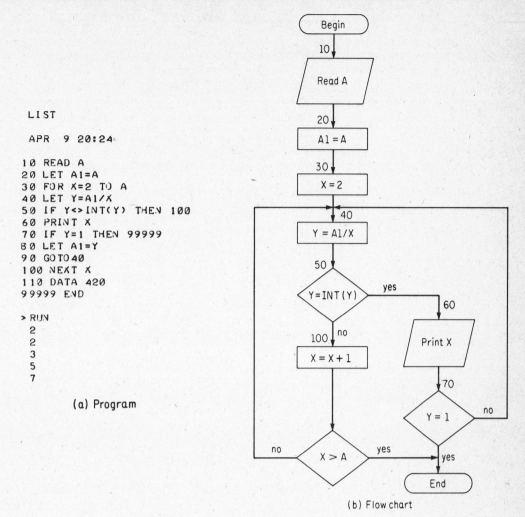

```
LIST

  APR  9  20:24

10 READ A
20 LET A1=A
30 FOR X=2 TO A
40 LET Y=A1/X
50 IF Y<>INT(Y) THEN 100
60 PRINT X
70 IF Y=1 THEN 99999
80 LET A1=Y
90 GOTO 40
100 NEXT X
110 DATA 420
99999 END

> RUN
  2
  2
  3
  5
  7
```

(a) Program

(b) Flow chart

Fig. 4-2. Program to determine the factors of a number.

would lead to a program with a few more statements than the one in Fig. 4-2, but the factors would be found with fewer calculations.

These modifications are left to the student to try if he so desires.

4-2. A Least-Squares Problem

Suppose we have a set of data consisting of N experimental observations consisting of the amount of fertilizer used per acre and the resulting yield of cotton per acre. A typical set might be as follows:

Observation	Fertilizer, lb/acre	Yield of Cotton, bales/acre
1	100	0.60
2	200	0.95
3	300	1.42
4	175	0.87
5	250	1.20
6	150	0.75

The independent variable X is the amount of fertilizer used per acre, and the dependent variable Y is the yield of cotton per acre. We would like to fit these observations to a straight line of the form

$$\hat{Y} = a + bX$$

where $\hat{Y}$ (pronounced "y hat") is the estimate of Y.

To do this, the procedure is as follows.

1. Compute the average of the observations on X,

$$\bar{X} = \left(\sum_{i=1}^{N} X_i \right) \bigg/ N$$

2. Compute the average of the observations on Y,

$$\bar{Y} = \left(\sum_{i=1}^{N} Y_i \right) \bigg/ N$$

3. Calculate the "corrected sum of squares,"

$$\sum_{i=1}^{N} x_i^2 = \sum_{i=1}^{N} X_i^2 - \frac{\bar{X}^2}{N}$$

4. Calculate the "corrected sum of cross-products,"

$$\sum_{i=1}^{N} x_i y_i = \sum_{i=1}^{N} X_i Y_i - \frac{\bar{X}\bar{Y}}{N}$$

5. Compute the coefficient b:

$$b = \frac{\displaystyle\sum_{i=1}^{N} x_i y_i}{\displaystyle\sum_{i=1}^{N} x_i^2}$$

6. Calculate the constant a:

$$a = \bar{Y} - b\bar{X}$$

Further relationships are available to ascertain the "goodness" of the fit, but the above equations are adequate for our purposes.

Consider preparation of a program to obtain a value for N followed by the observations from **DATA** statements, compute the coefficients a and b, and print the results. Just such a program is shown in Fig. 4-3 along with the flow chart. The program first reads (line 10) a value for N, the number of observations. Next (lines 20 through 50), the various sums are initialized to zero (variable **X1** is used for ΣX, variable **X2** for ΣX^2, **Y1** for ΣY, and **Y2** for ΣXY). A loop (lines 60 through 120) is then entered, and on each pass through the loop, a value for X and a value for Y are read, and the various sums updated. Lines 130 and 140 compute $\bar{X}$ and $\bar{Y}$, lines 150 and 160 compute Σx^2 and Σxy, and lines 170 and 180 compute the regression constants a and b, which are printed in line 190. For clarity, a separate **DATA** statement is used for the value of N, and a separate **DATA** statement is

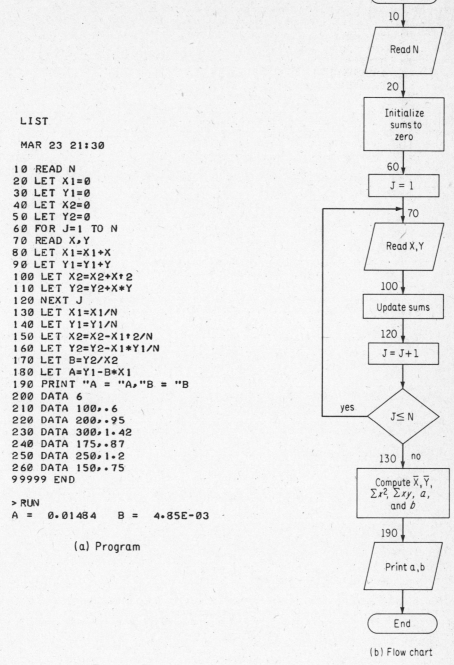

```
LIST

   MAR 23 21:30

10 READ N
20 LET X1=0
30 LET Y1=0
40 LET X2=0
50 LET Y2=0
60 FOR J=1 TO N
70 READ X,Y
80 LET X1=X1+X
90 LET Y1=Y1+Y
100 LET X2=X2+X↑2
110 LET Y2=Y2+X*Y
120 NEXT J
130 LET X1=X1/N
140 LET Y1=Y1/N
150 LET X2=X2-X1↑2/N
160 LET Y2=Y2-X1*Y1/N
170 LET B=Y2/X2
180 LET A=Y1-B*X1
190 PRINT "A = "A,"B = "B
200 DATA 6
210 DATA 100,.6
220 DATA 200,.95
230 DATA 300,1.42
240 DATA 175,.87
250 DATA 250,1.2
260 DATA 150,.75
99999 END

> RUN
A =   0.01484   B =   4.85E-03
```

(a) Program

(b) Flow chart

Fig. 4-3. Program to compute least-squares regression.

used for each observation pair. Of, course, all could have been entered in a single DATA statement.

4-3. Nested Loops

Suppose it is desired to determine the factors of the numbers from 420 to 425. The program in Fig. 4-2 can be used for this purpose provided it is run six times

```
LIST

   APR  9 20:22

   10 FOR A=420 TO 425
   20 PRINT "FACTORS OF" A
   30 LET A1=A
   40 FOR X=2 TO A
   50 LET Y=A1/X
   60 IF Y<>INT(Y) THEN 110
   70 PRINT X
   80 IF Y=1 THEN 120
   90 LET A1=Y
   100 GOTO 50
   110 NEXT X
   120 PRINT
   130 NEXT A
   99999 END

   > RUN
   FACTORS OF 420
      2
      2
      3
      5
      7

   FACTORS OF 421
      421

   FACTORS OF 422
      2
      211

   FACTORS OF 423
      3
      3
      47

   FACTORS OF 424
      2
      2
      2
      53

   FACTORS OF 425
      5
      5
      17
```

Outer Loop / Inner Loop

(a) Program

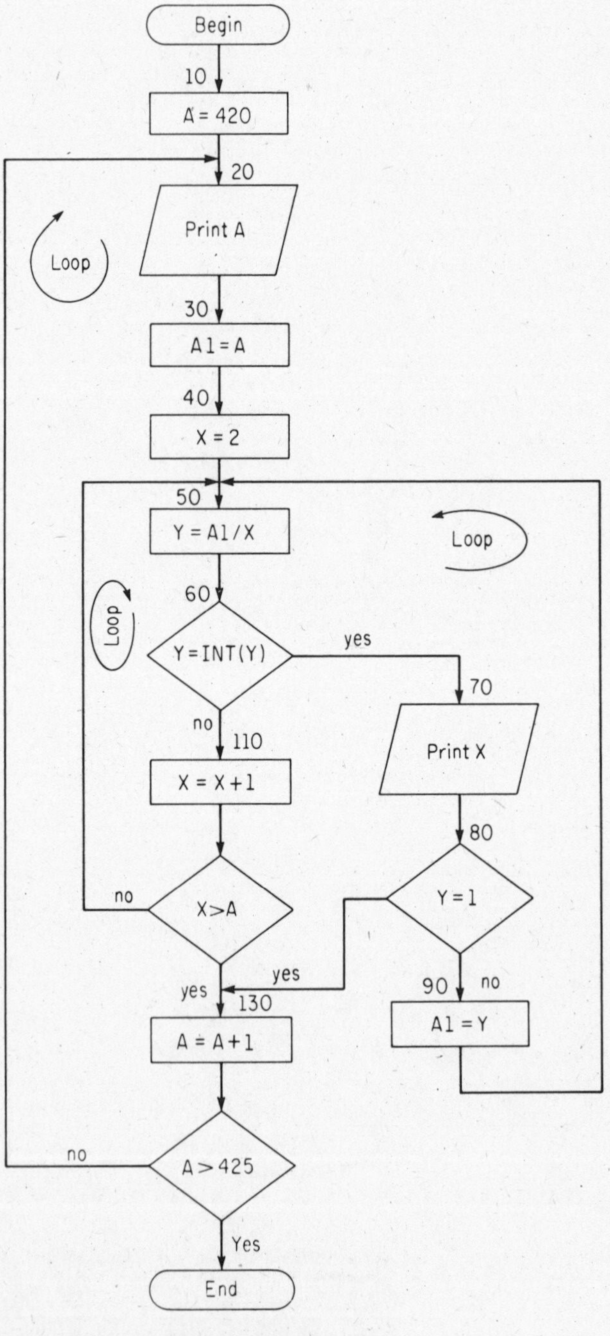

(b) Flow chart

Fig. 4-4. Illustration of nested loops.

with the appropriate changes in the **DATA** statement. Alternatively, the program could be made to return to the **READ** statement after factoring each number, and the six cases entered into a single **DATA** statement.

Another way to accomplish this is to use nested loops—that is, one loop inside the other. This is illustrated by the program in Fig. 4-4. Effectively what has been done is that the program in Fig. 4-2 has simply been placed inside another loop to form what is known as "nested" loops.

The **FOR** statement in line 10 initializes the value of **A** to 420, the first case that is to be run. Line 20 prints this value, and line 30 assigns variable **A1** the same value as **A**. The value of variable **A1** will vary within the inner loop, but **A** is not altered inside this loop. The next **FOR** statement is the beginning of the inner loop, which is identical to the loop in Fig. 4-2. However, note that upon detecting that the last factor has been located, the **IF-THEN** statement in line 80 transfers control to line 120, which is the **NEXT** statement corresponding to the outer loop.

The arrangement of nested loops must be such that they do not overlap or cross, i.e., no loop is partially outside of another loop. Figure 4-5 illustrates permis-

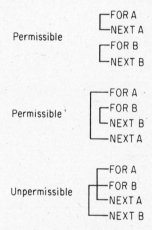

Fig. 4-5. Permissible and un-permissible arrangements of nested loops.

sible and unpermissible arrangements of nested loops. The variable or index used for a loop nested within another loop cannot be the same as the variable or index for the outer loop.

Actually, the program in Fig. 4-4 contains three loops, two of which are created by **FOR-NEXT** statements and one of which is created by the **GOTO** statement in line 100. These three loops are illustrated in the flow chart in Fig. 4-4b.

The program in Fig. 4-4 could be improved by incorporating the same modifications suggested for the program in Fig. 4-2. However, it should be noted that line 30, which assigns the value of **A** to variable **A1**, is necessary. If the value of **A** were changed, we would be modifying the value of the index within the **FOR-NEXT** loop, which is not allowed.

4-4. In Summary

The use of loops is so common in programming that a thorough under-standing of this programming feature is essential. The following exercises require the use of loops for efficient programming. The use of nested loops will be illus-trated by additional examples in the next chapter.

Exercises

4-1. A plant whose production rate is P lb/year produces a product whose value is V \$/lb. The product costs C \$/lb to produce. The gross profit is then $P \cdot (V-C)$. The total tax rate is 52%, so the profit after taxes is 0.48 times the gross profit. If the plant costs B \$ to build, the pay-out time in years is B divided by the profit after taxes.

Suppose the values of C, B, and P are known to be \$1.50/lb, \$900,000, and 200,000 lb/yr, respectively. Write a program to calculate the pay-out time for values of V from \$2.75/lb to \$3.25/lb in increments of \$0.05/lb. The listing should be in columnar fashion, with a value of V and a corre-sponding value of the pay-out time.

4-2. A man invests \$600 per year at 8% interest. How much will he have after ten years?

Write a BASIC program to calculate this using a loop. Read the amount invested annually, the interest rate, and how many years from now that the value of his investment is to be calculated.

4-3. At an interest rate of 6%, how much must you deposit at the first of each year so that at the end of five years you will have \$8,000?

Write a program to calculate this. Assume \$1.00 is deposited each year and calculate the amount available at the end of five years as per the previous program. The amount to be deposited is \$8,000 divided by this value. Read the interest rate, how much is to be accrued, and how many years deposits will be made.

4-4. One calculation frequently encountered in financial analyses is the com-putation of depreciation. One popular technique to do this is the sum-of-the-years-digits method. Suppose \$15,000 is to be depreciated over a 5 year period. The sum-of-the-years-digits is $1 + 2 + 3 + 4 + 5 = 15$. Accord-ing to this method, then 5/15 of \$15,000 is depreciated the first year, 4/15 the second, 3/15 the third, etc. Write a program that reads the amount to be depreciated and the number of years over which the depreciation is to be made. The output should be tabulated as follows for the above case:

1	5000.00
2	4000.00
3	3000.00
4	2000.00
5	1000.00

Run this program to calculate the annual depreciation if $50,000 is to be depreciated over ten years.

†4-5. Prepare a program to read N and calculate $N!$. N is always a nonnegative number, but may be zero ($0! = 1$). The output should be N and $N!$ [$N! = 1 \times 2 \times \cdots \times (N - 1) \times N$]. $N!$ is pronounced "N factorial."

4-6. In business applications, a quantity known as the capital-recovery factor is defined as follows:

$$\text{Capital-recovery factor} = \frac{i(1 + i)^n}{(1 + i)^n - 1}$$

where i is the interest rate and n is the number of years. Write a program to print a tabulated set of values for $n = 1$ through $n = 25$ for $i = 8\%$. The output should appear as follows:

1	1.08000
2	0.56077
3	0.38804
	etc.

4-7. A man borrows $100 at an interest rate of $1\frac{1}{2}\%$ per month. If he pays $10 at the end of each month, how much does he owe at the end of ten months? Write a program to solve this problem. Read the amount he borrows and the amount he pays each month. To be sure we are in agreement as to how the calculations are to be done, note that the interest for the first month is $0.015 \times \$100 = \$1.50$. Since he pays $10 at the end of the month, he owes $100 + \$1.50 - \$10 = \$91.50$. Use a loop to iterate these calculations for each month.

4-8. Evaluate the series

$$\sum_{n=0}^{20} \frac{1}{a + nb} = \frac{1}{a} + \frac{1}{a + b} + \frac{1}{a + 2b} + \frac{1}{a + 3b} + \cdots + \frac{1}{a + 20b}$$

for $a = 2$ and $b = 0.5$. Read a and b from a data statement, and write only the value of the sum.

4-9. On the interval $0 < X \leq 2$, log (X) can be represented by the following infinite series:

$$\log (X) = \frac{\left[(X - 1) - \frac{(X - 1)^2}{2} + \frac{(X - 1)^3}{3} - \cdots \right]}{2.302585} = \frac{\sum_{n=1}^{\infty} \frac{(-1)^{n-1}(X - 1)^n}{n}}{2.302585}$$

Prepare a program that reads a value for X and sums the series, printing the answer after 3, 5, 10, 50, and 100 terms. Also, print the answer using **LGT** for comparison. Run the program for $X = 1.8$. In programming, assume X will always be in the above interval.

†4-10. The binomial coefficients $\binom{n}{j}$ are given by the following expression:

$$\binom{n}{j} = \frac{n!}{j!(n - j)!}, \qquad j = 0, 1, \ldots, n$$

THE BINOMIAL COEFFICIENTS FOR N = 8

N	J	COEFFICIENT
8	0	1
8	1	8
8	2	28
8	3	56
8	4	70
8	5	56
8	6	28
8	7	8
8	8	1

Exercise 4-10.

Prepare a program to read a value for n (use $n = 8$ for this case), compute the binomial coefficients, and print the results as in the illustration. Assume n is always greater than 1. The cautious programmer will note that the first term is 1, and each succeeding term is simply $(n - j + 1)/j$, $j = 1, 2, \ldots, n$, times the preceding term. Programming in this manner avoids extremely large numbers which may occur if the factorials are evaluated directly. (This is not the case for $n = 8$, and such programming may be used if desired.)

4-11. The method known as "twenty questions" or "interval halving" is a simple, effective, and easy-to-program technique for finding roots of many poly-nomials. The method proceeds somewhat as follows:

Consider a function $f(x)$ similar to the function in the accompanying figure. The main feature is that the function has one and only one root on the interval (a, b). The root in this case can be found by the following technique:

1. Evaluate $f(x)$ at the midpoint of the interval, say $x = c = (a + b)/2$.

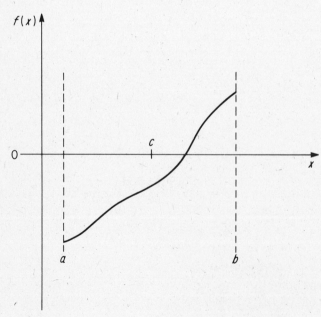

Exercise 4-11. Function suitable for "twenty questions."

2. If $f(c)$ is zero, the root is found. However, this is an extremely unlikely outcome.

3. If $f(c)$ is positive, note that the root must now lie on the interval (a, c). If $f(c)$ is negative, the root must lie on the interval (c, b). In either case, the interval on which the root is known to lie is cut in half.

4. The procedure is repeated for the new interval. As the interval is halved on each iteration, after twenty iterations the size of the interval is $1/2^{20}$, or negligibly small. After twenty iterations, the midpoint of the final interval is assumed to be the value of the root.

The function $f(x) = x^3 - x^2 - x - 1.9$ is very similar to the function shown in the accompanying sketch. Assuming a root lies between 0.0 and 5.0, use the method described above to locate the root.

4-12. Another technique for solving for roots of an equation is known as Newton's method. This technique proceeds as follows:

1. Assume a value, say $x = a$, for the root.
2. Evaluate $f(a)$. If $|f(a)| \leq \epsilon$, the root is found.
3. If not, evaluate $df(a)/dx = f'(a)$, the slope of the line tangent to $f(x)$ at $x = a$. This line is shown in the figure.
4. Determine the point b at which this tangent line intercepts the x-axis. This point is given by

$$b = a - f(a)/f'(a)$$

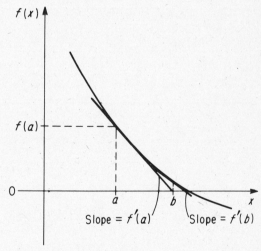

Exercise 4-12. Illustration of Newton's method.

5. The procedure is repeated from step 1 by assuming b as the new value for the root.

Prepare a program to perform these calculations for $f(x) = x^3 - x^2 - x - 1.9$. The input is to be a value for a and ϵ, and the output should be the root. Furthermore, the search will be terminated after twenty iterations with no output if the root has not been found. Let $a = 1.5$ and $\epsilon = 0.001$. What would happen if we selected $\epsilon = 0.000000001$?

Although this method will work for $f(x)$ given above, it is not difficult to find functions for which this iterative procedure diverges. For example, if $f'(a)$ were zero or nearly zero, problems arise.

4-13. Suppose the following equations are to be solved for x and y:

$$y = 1 - e^{-x}$$

$$y = x|x|$$

As we have two equations and two unknowns, they can be solved for x and y. Graphically, this is the problem of determining the intersection of the two curves in the illustration. Obviously, one could equate the two equations to obtain one equation in one unknown, but the result would be nonlinear and no advantage is accrued. Suppose the following procedure is implemented:

1. Let $y_1 = 1 - e^{-x}$ and $y_2 = x|x|$
2. Let $\delta = y_1 - y_2$
3. Assume a value for x, say b.
4. Compute y_1, y_2, and δ.
5. If $|\delta| \leq \epsilon$, the solution is found.
6. If not, note that when b is less than x_0 (the true solution), δ is positive. Now suppose b is increased by an amount proportional to δ, that is,

$$b = b + k\delta$$

(where k is a proportionality constant), and the procedure repeated from Step 4. The value for b should progressively approach x_0. Note also that this same equation can be applied when $b > x_0$, as the negative value of δ will cause a decrease in b.

Prepare a program to read a value for b, ϵ, and k, and print the value of b, ϵ, and k followed by values of b, y_1, y_2, and δ for *each interation*. Let

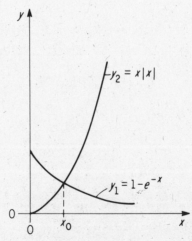

Exercise 4-13. Solution of nonlinear equations.

$b = 1., \epsilon = 0.001$, and run the program for values of k of 0.1, 0.5, 1, and 2. If convergence is not obtained after twenty iterations, abandon the search. Note that the difficulty with this technique is selecting the appropriate value for k, a small value requiring too many iterations and a large value producing an unstable situation.

4-14. The following definite integral

$$\int_0^2 (1 + X^2)\, dX = \int_0^2 f(X)\, dX$$

can be evaluated analytically to be 4.6667. However, not all integrals can be evaluated analytically. The purpose of this and the next few problems is to illustrate some of the features of numerical integration techniques.

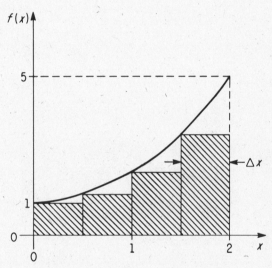

Exercise 4-14. Rectangular integration.

Perhaps the simplest of all numerical techniques is the rectangular approximation. The interval of integration is divided into smaller intervals, and the value of the function over the entire interval is assumed to be the value at either end. Graphically, this is shown in the illustration, using the value at the left end. The smooth curve is the plot of $1 + X^2$ vs. X, and the shaded area is the result of the numerical integration. The accuracy of the result increases as the number of intervals increases (width decreases).‡ The approximate value of the integral is

$$\int_0^2 (1 + X^2)\, dX \doteq \Delta X [f(0) + f(\Delta X) + f(2 \Delta X) + \cdots]$$

‡This is true up to a point. For very small intervals the round-off error may be serious.

Prepare a program to perform the following functions:

(a) Read the number of increments.

(b) Evaluate the integral numerically.

(c) Print the number of increments and the numerical result.

(d) Return to step (a) to repeat.

To illustrate the effect of increment size, run the program using 4, 10, 20, 50, 100, and 1000 increments.

†4-15. From an inspection of the accompanying figure, some improvement could possibly be obtained by evaluating the function at the midpoint of the increment. The result, as shown in the illustration, is given by

$$\int_0^2 (1 + X^2)\, dX \doteq \Delta X \left[f\left(\frac{\Delta X}{2}\right) + f\left(\frac{3\Delta X}{2}\right) + f\left(\frac{5\Delta X}{2}\right) + \cdots \right]$$

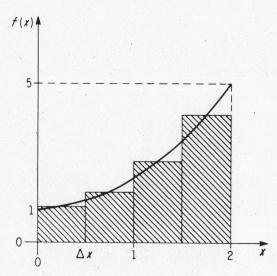

Exercise 4-15. Modification of rectangular integration.

Prepare a program similar to the one for Exercise 4-14, except use the illustrated technique. Again, evaluate using 4, 10, 20, 50, 100, and 1000 increments.

4-16. A slightly different scheme is to approximate the function by straight lines over a given increment, as shown in the drawing. In this case, the integral over the first increment would be $\Delta X \cdot [f(0) + f(\Delta X)]/2$. Summing over all increments yields the following equation, known as the trapezoid rule:

$$\int_0^2 (1 + X^2)\, dX$$
$$\doteq \Delta X \left[\frac{f(0)}{2} + f(\Delta X) + f(2\Delta X) + \cdots + f(2 - \Delta X) + \frac{f(2)}{2} \right]$$

Prepare a program similar to the one for Exercise 4-14 except use this integration technique. Again, evaluate using 4, 10, 20, 50, 100, and 1000 increments.

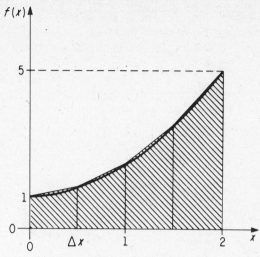

Exercise 4-16. Trapezoidal rule.

4-17. The digital computer is often called upon to solve differential equations numerically. Consider the following equation:

$$\frac{dc(t)}{dt} + c(t) = 1.$$

$$c(0) = 0$$

This equation with the specified initial condition is known to have the solution $c(t) = 1 - e^{-t}$, which can be used to compare with a numerical solution.

Consider the following scheme, known as the Euler technique:

(a) Solve the differential equation for the first derivative, yielding

$$\frac{dc(t)}{dt} = 1 - c(t)$$

(b) Select a time increment for the numerical integration.

(c) As $c(0)$ is known, $dc(0)/dt$, the initial slope, can be calculated.

(d) The point at the end of the first time increment is determined by assuming the derivative (or slope) is constant over the first time increment, as illustrated.

(e) This procedure is repeated for consecutive time increments, and is known as the Euler technique for solving ordinary differential equations.

Another way to obtain the same formulation is to approximate $dc(t)/dt$ by a forward difference, yielding

$$\frac{dc(t)}{dt} \doteq \frac{c(t + \Delta t) - c(t)}{\Delta t} = 1 - c(t)$$

Solving for $c(t + \Delta t)$ yields

$$c(t + \Delta t) = c(t) + [1 - c(t)]\Delta t$$

This recursive relationship is identical to the Euler technique.

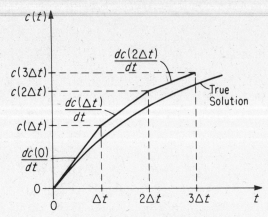

Exercise 4-17. Euler technique.

Prepare a program to use the above procedure to calculate the solution of the differential equation at $t = 1$. The program should read the number of increments to be used, and write as output the number of increments, the numerical solution, and true solution. Determine these for 4, 10, 20, 50, 100, and 1000 increments.

4-18. The Euler technique can be modified slightly to obtain some improvement. The procedure is as follows:

(a) Evaluate the derivative at the beginning of the increment, i.e., $c'(t)$.

(b) Using this slope, determine a first estimate of $c(t + \Delta t)$, say $g(t + \Delta t)$. Note that $g(t + \Delta t) = c(t) + (\Delta t) c'(t)$.

(c) Now evaluate the slope at the end of the increment, i.e., $g'(t + \Delta t)$, using the original differential equation with g substituted for c.

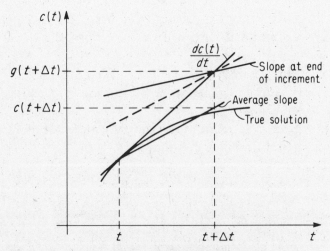

Exercise 4-18. Modified Euler technique.

(d) Average the slopes determined in steps (a) and (c), and use this value to determine $c(t + \Delta t)$ by the equation

$$c(t + \Delta t) = c(t) + (\Delta t)[c'(t) + g'(t + \Delta t)]/2$$

This technique, illustrated below, is known as the modified Euler technique. Repeat Exercise 4-17 using this technique.

4-19. Probably the most popular high-order integration technique is a fourth-order Runge-Kutta. Let the differential equation be of the form $dc(t)/dt = f[t,c(t)]$, where $c(t)$ is the dependent variable and t is the independent variable. Then the point $c(t + \Delta t)$ at a small increment Δt from a known point $c(t)$ is given by

$$c(t + \Delta t) = c(t) + (\Delta t)(K_1 + 2K_2 + 2K_3 + K_4)/6$$

$$K_1 = f[t, c(t)]$$

$$K_2 = f\left[t + \frac{\Delta t}{2}, c(t) + \frac{K_1 \Delta t}{2}\right]$$

$$K_3 = f\left[t + \frac{\Delta t}{2}, c(t) + \frac{K_2 \Delta t}{2}\right]$$

$$K_4 = f[t + \Delta t, c(t) + K_3 \Delta t]$$

Use this procedure to solve the differential equation in Exercise 4-17.

4-20. The above methods for numerically solving first-order differential equations can be readily extended to higher-order differential equations. For example, consider the following equation:

$$\frac{d^2c(t)}{dt^2} + \frac{dc(t)}{dt} + c(t) = 1$$

$$c(0) = 0$$

$$\frac{dc(0)}{dt} = 0$$

Define a new variable, say $z(t)$, as follows:

$$\frac{dc(t)}{dt} = z(t) \qquad\qquad\qquad \text{(a)}$$

Now the original equation becomes

$$\frac{dz(t)}{dt} + z(t) + c(t) = 1 \qquad\qquad\qquad \text{(b)}$$

The boundary conditions are

$$c(0) = 0$$
$$z(0) = 0$$

Now equations (a) and (b) are first-order differential equations and can be solved simultaneously using the concepts presented in the previous exercises. Using the Euler technique, the iterative equations are:

$$c(t + \Delta t) = c(t) + (\Delta t)[z(t)]$$
$$z(t + \Delta t) = z(t) + (\Delta t)[1 - z(t) - c(t)]$$

Prepare a program to solve the above differential equation for $c(4)$. Let the input be the number of increments, and solve for 4, 10, 20, 50, 100, and 1000 increments.

Chapter 5

ARRAYS

The use of subscripted variables or arrays permits the programmer to conveniently structure programs to perform repetitive computations on large quantities of data. Coupled with the **FOR-NEXT** statements, these features form the most powerful combination of statements available in BASIC.

This chapter begins with a discussion of how the computer stores and retrieves data. A thorough understanding of this will be of invaluable assistance in understanding the use of arrays. We shall then consider one-dimensional arrays, or lists, followed by a discussion of two-dimensional arrays or tables.

5-1. Memory Allocation

Between receipt of a BASIC program and the printing of answers, the computer passes through two distinct phases. The first phase is compilation, where the computer decodes the BASIC statements, places them in the proper sequence, generates elementary machine-executable instructions,‡ and assigns storage locations for the variables and constants in the program. During this phase certain error messages are generated, indicating that the programmer has not followed the rules of the BASIC language.

During the execution phase of the program, the indicated computations are performed. Values are assigned to variables in **READ** and **LET** statements, decisions are made, and answers are printed. Of course, some errors are generated in this phase, usually indicating a fault in the program logic.

Let's consider the compilation phase a little more closely, specifically the allocation of storage locations to variables and constants. Consider the statement

$$\text{LET} \quad A = 2$$

The BASIC compiler establishes two storage locations, one for the variable A and one for the constant 2. The value 2 is stored in the location reserved for the constant, but nothing is stored in the location reserved for **A** until this statement is executed during execution.

Now consider the program on p. 74.

---

‡Many BASIC systems are implemented as interpreters, which do not generate machine executable instructions but instead re-decode a statement each time it is to be executed.

```
10 READ A,B
20 LET C=A*B+2/A
30 PRINT A,B,C
40 DATA 1,4
99999 END
```

One storage location is needed for the constant 2 in line 20, and three locations are needed for the variables A, B, and C. The sequence is not alphabetical, but according to the order of occurrence in the program. Most systems allocate storage locations for all variables in consecutive locations in the computer's memory.

Now suppose storage locations are to be reserved for the variables A, B, X1, X2, X3, X4, D, and J. A reasonable arrangement might be as follows:

Storage Location	Variable
1000	A
1001	B
1002	X1
1003	X2
1004	X3
1005	X4
1006	D
1007	J

Suppose X1 is the age of a couple's first child, X2 the age of the second child, X3 the third, and X4 the fourth. We have effectively stored a list in the computer's memory, namely the list of the ages of a couple's children.

In this example we have named a simple variable corresponding to the age of each child. As we shall see later, it will usually be more convenient to give the list a name, and store and retrieve elements in the list according to their position within the list. For example, suppose we call our list X. As we shall see in the next section, the position within the list is denoted by a subscript enclosed in parentheses. That is, X(2) will denote the second element in the list.

Our storage locations would now be arranged as follows:

Storage Location	Variable
1000	A
1001	B
1002	X(1)
1003	X(2)
1004	X(3)
1005	X(4)
1006	D
1007	J

It is now possible to use FOR-NEXT statements to operate on these elements consecutively. For example, the statements

```
FOR  J=1  TO  4
PRINT  X(J)
NEXT  J
```

would print the ages of all the children.

Let's assume for the moment that zero subscripts are not allowed. Then to be able to access every element in the list, the computer needs to remember the storage location just prior to the first element in the list. For the above example, this would be location 1001. The numerical value of the subscript is added to this value to obtain the address of the desired element of the list. For example, to retrieve X(2) we add 2 to 1001 to obtain 1003, the location of the second element.

Recall that the allocation of variable storage occurs during compile time. Therefore, in order for the compiler to assign a storage location for the variable D, it must somehow know how many elements are in the list. This must be explicitly specified in order for compilation to proceed. We shall see that BASIC assumes ten elements unless told otherwise by a special statement, called a *dimension statement*. Since this specification must be made at compile time, the size (or dimension) of the list cannot be read or computed during execution.

It should be pointed out at this point that the storage of lists can consume a significant portion of the computer's storage area. The good programmer will store a list only if absolutely necessary. Generally, if the elements in the list are used only once, it is not necessary to store them. If they are needed on two or more occasions, the alternative is to store them or read them in each time they are needed. In this case, storage of the list is preferred if the space is available.

We shall now examine the rules of BASIC for one-dimensional arrays or lists, reserving two-dimensional arrays or tables until later in the chapter.

5-2. One-Dimensional Array or List

To illustrate the concept of a one-dimensional array or list, consider the tabulation of a single statistic on the students in a class. Suppose we first assign each student a number, beginning with one and numbering consecutively. If the statistic is the student's age, we could present this statistic in the following fashion:

Student Number	Age
1	22
2	19
3	29
4	20
5	25
6	23
7	22

To enter this information into the computer, two avenues are open to us. First, we could assign an individual variable name to each entry. For example, we might let A1 represent the age of the first student, A2 the second, and so forth. The second approach would be to assign a single name to the entire list, and retrieve entries according to their position in the list. That is, the first position in the list would logically correspond to the age of student number 1, the second position to student number 2, etc. As we shall see, this latter alternative is by far the more convenient.

In BASIC, a single letter of the alphabet is used to form the name of an array, giving a total of 26 possibilities. Thus, we might choose to use array **A** for the list of students' ages as discussed in the previous paragraph. The position in the array is denoted by a "subscript" which is actually on the line but enclosed in parentheses. That is, $A(1)$ is the first element, $A(2)$ is the second, etc. For example, if array **A** is the list given earlier in this section, the statement

$$X = A(5)$$

would cause the value 25 to be assigned to the variable **X**.

It is also permissible to use a variable or an expression as a subscript, e.g.,

$$A(2*J + K)$$

The values of **J** and **K**, which must have been defined previously in the program, are used to evaluate the expression, thus obtaining a numerical value which must be a positive number greater than or equal to one.‡ If this value is not an integer, the fractional part is truncated. That is, we are talking about the first element of the array, the second element, and so on, not about element 1.720401.

To illustrate the use of a variable as a subscript, suppose **J** has been assigned the value 4 earlier in the program. The statement

$$X = A(J)$$

would cause the value 20 to be assigned to **X**. If **I** were assigned the value -1, then the value of $A(I + J)$ would be 29.

To illustrate the use of arrays, the program in Fig. 5-1 simply reads a list from the **DATA** statement and prints it. Note the use of a loop containing the **READ** statement to read element 1, then element 2, etc., through element 7. At this point, array **A** contains seven values, any of which may be retrieved by referencing the

```
LIST

MAR 23 21:18

10 REM INPUT SECTION
20 FOR J=1 TO 7
30 READ A(J)
40 NEXT J
50 REM OUTPUT SECTION
60 FOR K=1 TO 7
70 PRINT A(K)
80 NEXT K
90 DATA 22,19,29,20,25,23,22
99999 END

>RUN
  22
  19
  29
  20
  25
  23
  22
```

Fig. 5-1. Illustration of use of arrays.

‡An exception to this is discussed in Sec. 5-3.

proper position within the array. Note that the input statements would be virtually identical regardless of the size of the array.

The output section of the program is virtually identical to the input section. Note that K is used as the index of the loop, whereas J was used for the loop containing the READ statement. Although J (or K) could have been used in both loops, a different index was used in this example to emphasize that A(J) and A(K) refer to the *same* array; that is, array A. The subscript merely specifies the position within the array.

The program in Fig. 5-1 is equivalent to the following program:

```
10  READ A(1),A(2),A(3),A(4),A(5),A(6),A(7)
20  PRINT A(1)
30  PRINT A(2)
40  PRINT A(3)
50  PRINT A(4)
60  PRINT A(5)
70  PRINT A(6)
80  PRINT A(7)
90  DATA 22,19,29,20,25,23,22
99999 END
```

This example is an attempt to illustrate that the array consists of seven distinct elements, each stored in a separate storage location. The array is designated by a single name, i.e., A, plus a subscript to specify the relative location within the array. Since the name is the same for all elements, they can be retrieved, operated on, or stored one at a time using a loop to vary the subscript from one up to the maximum position within the array.

As the second illustration of the use of an array, suppose we are to prepare a program to read our list of the ages of students, compute the average age, print the average age, and print in tabular form the student number, his age, and the difference between his age and the average age. The program and its flow chart are shown in Fig. 5-2. The first step (line 10) is to initialize a sum. A loop is used to read the successive ages and add them to the sum. The average age is calculated (line 60) and printed (line 70). After printing the headings, a loop is used to print for each student his number, his age, and the difference from the average.

In this example, it would not be necessary to use an array if the differences from the average were not to be calculated. Calculation of the average of a group of numbers was a part of the least-squares program in Fig. 4-3, which does not utilize an array.

5-3. The DIM Statement

For simple variables, the BASIC compiler reserves only one storage location, i.e., room in memory where the value of the variable can be stored for later use. For arrays, life is not so simple, since the array may be composed of one element, five elements, a hundred elements, or whatever is needed. BASIC must somehow

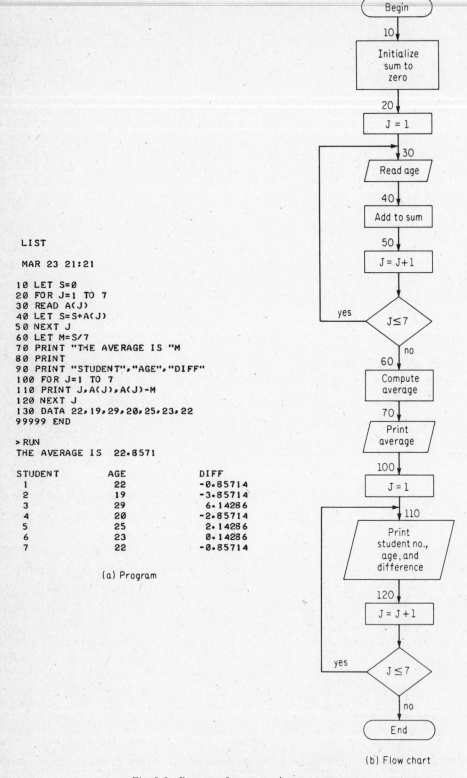

```
LIST

  MAR 23 21:21

10 LET S=0
20 FOR J=1 TO 7
30 READ A(J)
40 LET S=S+A(J)
50 NEXT J
60 LET M=S/7
70 PRINT "THE AVERAGE IS "M
80 PRINT
90 PRINT "STUDENT","AGE","DIFF"
100 FOR J=1 TO 7
110 PRINT J,A(J),A(J)-M
120 NEXT J
130 DATA 22,19,29,20,25,23,22
99999 END

> RUN
THE AVERAGE IS  22.8571

STUDENT        AGE          DIFF
   1           22          -0.85714
   2           19          -3.85714
   3           29           6.14286
   4           20          -2.85714
   5           25           2.14286
   6           23           0.14286
   7           22          -0.85714
```

(a) Program

(b) Flow chart

Fig. 5-2. Program for computing average.

know the maximum number of elements in the array. This number must be either defined explicitly or implied.

Unless told otherwise, BASIC automatically reserves ten storage locations for a one-dimensional array. To see why this is necessary, it is helpful to examine a program to see what storage locations are required. For the program in Fig. 5-2, the following variables are used:

line 10   S, simple variable (one storage location)
line 20   J, simple variable (one storage location)
line 30   A, one-dimensional array, implied to contain ten elements
line 60   M, simple variable (one storage location)

These can be visualized as being "strung out" in the available storage area, appearing as

S   J   A(1)   A(2)   ...   A(10)   M

In order for the computer to determine where to store M for this program, it must know the size (i.e., number of elements) of the array A.

If the array contains more than ten elements, a DIM statement must be used to inform the compiler to reserve more storage locations for the array. The format of the DIM statement is

DIM   *letter (integer)*,   *letter (integer)*,   etc.

Each *letter* is the single-letter name of the array whose size is being specified, and *integer* (or dimension) is the number of storage locations to be reserved. For example, the statement

10   DIM   A(15),   G(25)

reserves 15 storage locations for array A and 25 storage locations for array G. Some systems place an upper limit on the maximum size of an array, a typical limit being 1022.

In the DIM statement, the size or dimension of the array must be specified by an *integer number*. This is because the storage locations are established at *compile* time, i.e., when the computer is translating the BASIC statements into machine-executable instructions. A common mistake made by a beginning programmer is to attempt to use the following statements or their equivalent:

10   LET   J = 20
20   DIM   A(J)

These are unacceptable in most systems because J is undefined at compile time. It is not assigned the value of 20 until line 10 is *executed* subsequent to completion of the compilation.

In all examples presented so far, the DIM statement has been used to increase the size of the array beyond the implied size of ten. However, the DIM statement may also be used to reduce the size of the array. For example, the statement

10   DIM   A(6)

reserves only six storage locations for array A. The only reason for using this statement is to conserve storage locations. There is no harm in using arrays known to be too large unless the program requires more storage locations than are available. This aspect is more important for the two-dimensional arrays discussed in Sec. 5-6.

A program may contain more than one DIM statement, but a given array may appear in only one DIM statement. Many BASIC compilers accept these statements anywhere in the program, but most programmers tend to place these statements near the beginning of the program. Some compilers require that the DIM statement appear prior to the first appearance of the array in the program. Always placing DIM statements first in the program certainly meets this requirement.

5-4. Use of a Zero Subscript

In our earlier discussions, we stated that the value of the subscript must be a positive integer number. On some systems, the subscript may also assume the value of zero. That is, the array dimensioned by the statement

$$10 \quad \text{DIM} \quad \text{A(4)}$$

consists of the elements

$$\text{A(0)} \quad \text{A(1)} \quad \text{A(2)} \quad \text{A(3)} \quad \text{A(4)}$$

or a total of five elements. For certain types of problems, this feature can be extremely useful, while for other problems it is of virtually no value and results in the loss of one storage location. Consequently, some systems have incorporated this feature while others have not.

The only alternative in a general manual of this type is to point out that such a feature exists on some systems, but take the conservative or "safe" version in the remainder of the discussion. Suppose you have written a program that does not use zero subscripts. It would, of course, run on all systems. However, if you write a program using a zero subscript, it will run on only those systems that reserve the extra storage location. In this manual, we shall write programs as if zero subscripts are not allowed.

5-5. Examples Using Subscripts

Inventory Program. One popular use for a computer is to maintain an up-to-date account of items in inventory. Suppose the status of the inventory at the beginning of the month is available, and will be entered via DATA statements containing the stock number followed by the number in inventory. To limit these statements to a reasonable number, we shall write a program to handle only six items. The first section of the program in Fig. 5-3 enters this information into arrays S (for stock number) and Q (for quantity in inventory).

Furthermore, suppose we prepare DATA statements giving the stock number for each item received followed by the quantity received. Stock numbers may

```
LIST

MAR 23 21:16

10 REM READ INITIAL INVENTORY
20 FOR J=1 TO 6
30 READ S(J),Q(J)
40 NEXT J
50 REM UPDATE INVENTORY FOR STOCK RECEIVED
60 READ S1,Q1
70 IF S1=0 THEN 130
80 FOR J=1 TO 6
90 IF S1<>S(J) THEN 110
100 LET Q(J)=Q(J)+Q1
110 NEXT J
120 GOTO60
130 REM UPDATE INVENTORY FOR STOCK SHIPPED
140 READ S1,Q1
150 IF S1=0 THEN 210
160 FOR J=1 TO 6
170 IF S1<>S(J) THEN 190
180 LET Q(J)=Q(J)-Q1
190 NEXT J
200 GOTO140
210 REM WRITE FINAL INVENTORY
220 PRINT "STOCK NO.","QUANTITY"
230 FOR J=1 TO 6
240 PRINT S(J),Q(J)
250 NEXT J
260 DATA 1207,12,1049,1,0907,5,0412,0,1222,7,0015,2
270 DATA 0412,5,0015,3,1049,7,1222,5,0412,5,0015,2,0,0
280 DATA 1207,2,1049,3,1222,10,0015,4,0412,7,0,0
99999 END

>RUN
STOCK NO.       QUANTITY
1207             10
1049              5
907               5
412               3
1222              2
15                3
```

(a) Program

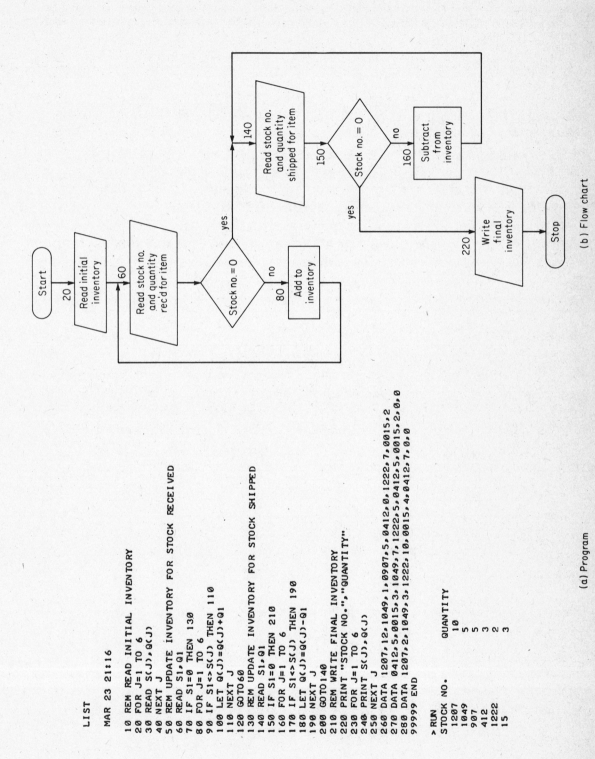

(b) Flow chart

Fig. 5-3. Inventory program.

appear in random order. Depending upon the shipments, a specific stock number may appear more than once, or may not appear at all. Also, the number of shipments received varies, so the **DATA** statement will be terminated with two zero entries. Upon detecting these, the computer will proceed to the stock shipped section of the program. The second section of the program in Fig. 5-3 embodies this logic.

As illustrated by the third section of the program in Fig. 5-3, the stock shipped is treated in the same manner as the stock received. The final section prints the new inventory.

In practice, the old inventory would be stored in a file. The information on stock received and stock shipped may also be in a file, or perhaps on paper tape. After updating the old inventory, the program would store the new inventory in a file as well as printing it. These aspects are discussed further in Sec. 6-5.

The program in Fig. 5-3 could be improved in two ways. First, once we have found the appropriate element in stock and incremented the quantity in stock in line 100, we could transfer to line 60 rather than remain in the loop. A similar improvement could be made after line 180. Second, if a stock number is read which does not correspond to an element of array **S**, the entry is ignored. This would not be a desirable characteristic of a practical inventory program.

Arranging Elements in Ascending Order. If an array contains a large number of entries, specific entries can often be found more easily if the elements are in ascending (i.e., smallest element first) or descending order. Consider writing a program to read an array, arrange the elements in ascending order, and print. Suppose our array contains the elements 4.1, 9.2, 6.9, 1.7, 1.2, in that order.

Consider preparing the statements to arrange the elements in ascending order. Suppose we first begin by locating the smallest element in the array. We can assume it is the first element, and then examine each of the remaining elements, updating our assumption as necessary. The BASIC statements to do this are

```
100 LET M=1
110 FOR J=2 TO 5
120 IF A(M)<A(J) THEN 140
130 LET M=J
140 NEXT J
```

After executing these statements, the value of M equals 2 for our example. We must now place element M in position 1. But since we cannot discard element 1, we must put it into element M. This is accomplished with the following three statements using an additional variable T:

```
150 LET T=A(M)
160 LET A(M)=A(1)
170 LET A(1)=T
```

Upon completion of these statements, our array consists of the elements 1.2, 9.2, 6.9, 1.7, and 4.1.

Next we must examime elements 2 through 5, repeating the above procedure. That is, assume element 2 is smallest, and search over the remaining elements.

The appropriate statements are

```
100 LET M=2
110 FOR J=3 TO 5
120 IF A(M)<A(J) THEN 140
130 LET M=J
140 NEXT J
```

In this case, the result is M equal to 4. Interchanging elements 2 and M with the statements

```
150 LET T=A(M)
160 LET A(M)=A(2)
170 LET A(2)=T
```

gives the array 1.2, 1.7, 6.9, 9.2, and 4.1.

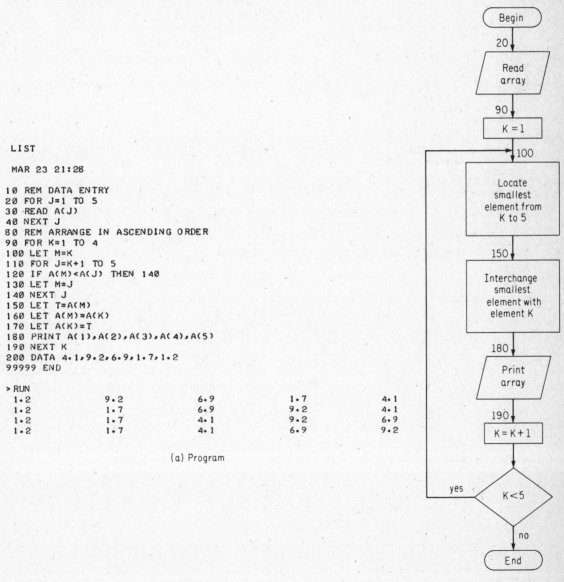

```
LIST

 MAR 23 21:28

10 REM DATA ENTRY
20 FOR J=1 TO 5
30 READ A(J)
40 NEXT J
80 REM ARRANGE IN ASCENDING ORDER
90 FOR K=1 TO 4
100 LET M=K
110 FOR J=K+1 TO 5
120 IF A(M)<A(J) THEN 140
130 LET M=J
140 NEXT J
150 LET T=A(M)
160 LET A(M)=A(K)
170 LET A(K)=T
180 PRINT A(1),A(2),A(3),A(4),A(5)
190 NEXT K
200 DATA 4.1,9.2,6.9,1.7,1.2
99999 END

> RUN
1.2          9.2          6.9          1.7          4.1
1.2          1.7          6.9          9.2          4.1
1.2          1.7          4.1          9.2          6.9
1.2          1.7          4.1          6.9          9.2
```

(a) Program

(b) Flow chart

Fig. 5-4. Arranging elements of an array in ascending order.

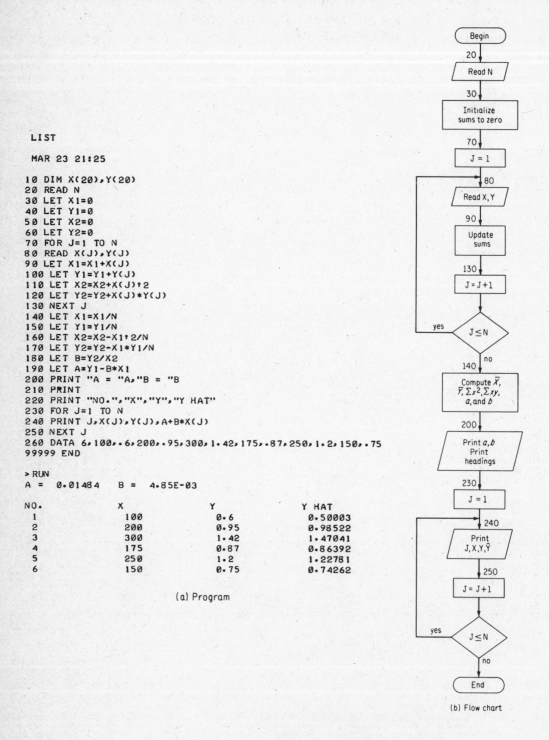

```
LIST

 MAR 23 21:25

10 DIM X(20),Y(20)
20 READ N
30 LET X1=0
40 LET Y1=0
50 LET X2=0
60 LET Y2=0
70 FOR J=1 TO N
80 READ X(J),Y(J)
90 LET X1=X1+X(J)
100 LET Y1=Y1+Y(J)
110 LET X2=X2+X(J)↑2
120 LET Y2=Y2+X(J)*Y(J)
130 NEXT J
140 LET X1=X1/N
150 LET Y1=Y1/N
160 LET X2=X2-X1↑2/N
170 LET Y2=Y2-X1*Y1/N
180 LET B=Y2/X2
190 LET A=Y1-B*X1
200 PRINT "A = ",A,"B = "B
210 PRINT
220 PRINT "NO.","X","Y","Y HAT"
230 FOR J=1 TO N
240 PRINT J,X(J),Y(J),A+B*X(J)
250 NEXT J
260 DATA 6,100,.6,200,.95,300,1.42,175,.87,250,1.2,150,.75
99999 END

> RUN
A =   0.01484    B =   4.85E-03

NO.          X             Y             Y HAT
  1          100           0.6           0.50003
  2          200           0.95          0.98522
  3          300           1.42          1.47041
  4          175           0.87          0.86392
  5          250           1.2           1.22781
  6          150           0.75          0.74262
```

(a) Program

(b) Flow chart

Fig. 5-5. Revised least-squares program.

Obviously we must repeat this procedure again. Since the smallest of the last three elements is element 5, we interchange elements 3 and 5 to obtain the array 1.2, 1.7, 4.1, 9.2, and 6.9. Now only two elements remain to be ordered. Interchanging them gives the array 1.2, 1.7, 4.1, 6.9, and 9.2 in ascending order.

The program and flow chart in Fig. 5-4 illustrate implementation of this procedure using two nested loops. Note that only four iterations (one less than the number of elements) of the outer loop are required. A print statement to print the entire array has been inserted into the outer loop so that the ordering process may be followed.

Least-Squares Fit. The last example will be an extension of the least squares problem discussed in Sec. 4-2. In the program presented in Fig. 4-3, the observations X and Y were not stored in arrays, since the values were read, used once, and never needed again. However, suppose it is desired to provide some additional output consisting of the observation number, the value of the independent variable X, the observed value of the dependent variable Y, and the estimate of the dependent variable $\hat{Y}$ computed using the regression equation. Since the constants a and b in the regression equation cannot be calculated until after all data has been read, the values of X and Y must now be stored in arrays.

The revised BASIC program and its flow chart are shown in Fig. 5-5. This program is virtually identical to the one in Fig. 4-3 except for the following:

1. The **DIM** statement in line 10 specifies that arrays **X** and **Y** consist of twenty elements each. Although this statement is not needed for the example solved, the same program could be used for other problems by simply changing the **DATA** statement.
2. Values of X and Y are stored in the respective arrays in line 80.
3. The **PRINT** statement in line 240 requires that values of X and Y be retrieved from the array for printing and for calculating $\hat{Y}$.

Although arrays for X and Y could have been used in the program in Fig. 4-3, this is not necessary and should generally be avoided if possible.

5-6. Two-Dimensional Arrays or Tables‡

The concept and use of lists in BASIC is readily extended to tables, or more elegantly, two-dimensional arrays. Like lists, tables are also denoted by a single letter of the alphabet, but the letter is followed by two subscripts enclosed in parentheses and separated by a comma.

The usual convention is to let the first subscript designate the number of the row and the second subscript designate the number of the column, as illustrated for the following table:

‡The student should probably attempt an exercise or two using one-dimensional arrays before attempting this section.

College Enrollment

Year	Bachelor	Master	Doctorate	
1960	4,976	472	78	(row 1)
1961	5,122	520	80	(row 2)
1962	6,906	541	91	(row 3)
1963	7,809	609	92	(row 4)
1964	8,107	623	107	(row 5)
1965	7,920	647	117	(row 6)
1966	8,019	659	128	(row 7)
	(column 1)	(column 2)	(column 3)	

This is rather arbitrary, but we shall adhere to it in this manual. Using this convention, element T(2,3) is the element in the second row and third column of Table T. The statements

```
100 FOR K=1 TO 3
110 FOR J=1 TO 7
120 READ T(J,K)
130 NEXT J
140 NEXT K
```

read the elements of table T column by column. Similarly, the statements

```
100 FOR J=1 TO 7
110 FOR K=1 TO 3
120 READ T(J,K)
130 NEXT K
140 NEXT J
```

read the elements of table T row by row.

As for one-dimensional arrays, the implied size of a two-dimensional array is 10 rows and 10 columns, or a total of 100 elements (121 if zero subscripts are recognized). The size may be increased or decreased by using a DIM statement. Since the statement

$$\text{DIM} \quad T(3,4)$$

reduces the size of array T from 100 elements to 12 elements (a savings of 88 storage locations), it is here that significant savings in storage space can be gained by using DIM statements for small arrays. Of course, a DIM statement may contain both tables and lists (a list is really a table with only one column).

Figure 5-6 illustrates a program that reads a table T from DATA statements and computes the sum of each column, storing the results in list S. The table is summed column by column by using an outer loop consisting of the FOR and NEXT statements in lines 80 and 130. Line 90 initializes the proper element of list S to zero. The inner loop consisting of the FOR and NEXT statements in lines 100 and 120 simply adds the values of T in the specified column to the proper element of S. Line 140 prints the sum of each column of the table.

In this example, the only justification for using an array for S is so that the output could all be on the same line. If it were acceptable to write the sums one under the other, the sum of a column could be printed as it is computed, thereby

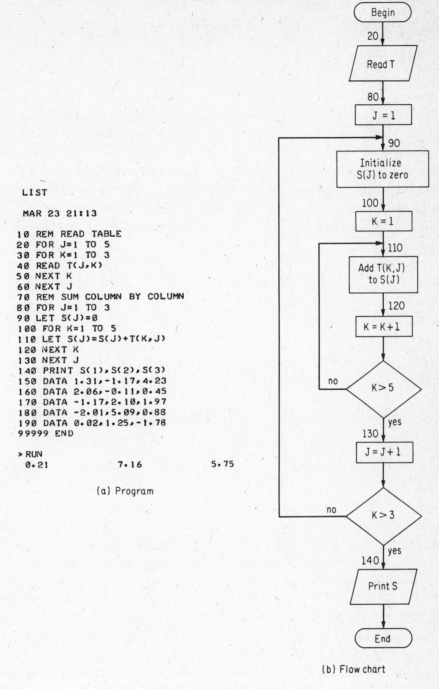

```
LIST

MAR 23 21:13

10 REM READ TABLE
20 FOR J=1 TO 5
30 FOR K=1 TO 3
40 READ T(J,K)
50 NEXT K
60 NEXT J
70 REM SUM COLUMN BY COLUMN
80 FOR J=1 TO 3
90 LET S(J)=0
100 FOR K=1 TO 5
110 LET S(J)=S(J)+T(K,J)
120 NEXT K
130 NEXT J
140 PRINT S(1),S(2),S(3)
150 DATA 1.31,-1.17,4.23
160 DATA 2.06,-0.11,0.45
170 DATA -1.17,2.10,1.97
180 DATA -2.01,5.09,0.88
190 DATA 0.02,1.25,-1.78
99999 END

> RUN
0.21          7.16          5.75
```

(a) Program

(b) Flow chart

Fig. 5-6. Summing columns of a table.

obviating any need for an array. In Chapter 6 on input/output, we shall discuss a means whereby the sums can appear on one line and still not use an array for S.

5-7. In Summary

The use of lists and tables is without question one of the more important features of BASIC programming, since they permit the handling of large quantities of information with the minimum of programming effort. The programmer should make every effort to gain facility in using this feature.

Exercises‡

5-1. Twenty students take an exam on which the marks are from 0 to 100. Write a program to determine how many students make a mark higher than the average. Write out the array of marks and the number earning a mark higher than the average. Make up some trial data.

5-2. The accounting procedure at the typical computer center consists of assigning a charge number to each user, which he must submit with each job. Suppose at the end of each job, the computer records the user's charge number and the time of the run in minutes. Write a program that reads this data and calculates the total amount of time used by each user on all jobs he ran. The output should be in columnar fashion with user number, total time used, and per cent of total. Use a zero entry to indicate end-of-data. Input data are

User No.	Time
40709	1.27
80001	2.34
50200	2.11
40709	4.02
40201	3.11
70207	2.06
50200	3.09
80001	1.02
40709	0.79
70207	3.04

5-3. Consider preparation of a program to calculate telephone bills. Our booming company has ten customers, whose identification numbers and base charges are available from a **DATA** statement. In addition, we have several records containing charges for each long distance call made along with the customer number of the calling party. Of course, a given customer may make no calls or several calls. The records for long distance are neither counted nor ordered. Write a program to compute and print the total charges for each customer. Don't forget to add 10% federal excise tax for long-distance calls, but remember that base charges are not taxable. Enter the base charges first, making up your own data.

5-4. Suppose the sales slips on merchandise sold in a given department contain the amount of the sale and the salesperson's identification number. We would like to prepare a program to calculate (1) the total sales of each salesperson, (2) the percent of the total, and (3) his or her commission for the day (3% of the sales above $50). These sales slips are neither

‡*Caution*: Not all exercises require use of arrays.

counted nor ordered in any way, and are to be entered into the program via **DATA** statements in the same sequence. The program's output should be in columns containing the salesperson's identification number, the total amount of his or her sales for the day, the per cent of the total, and his or her commission. Make up your own data.

†**5-5.** Modify Exercise 4-6 to calculate the capital-recovery factor for interest rates of 2%, 4%, 6%, 8%, and 10% for a given year. The output should be six columns, one column for the year and one column for the capital-recovery factor at each interest rate. The year should be read from a **DATA** statement, and construct the program to do these calculations for as many entries as in the **DATA** statements.

5-6. Suppose we are given a set of observations consisting of values of the independent variable x (perhaps the age of a child) and corresponding values of the dependent variable y (perhaps the weight of the child). This data might appear as follows:

x	y
3	31
5	61
2	27
7	75
9	102

Suppose also that it is anticipated that this data should follow an equation of the type $y = ax + b$, where a and b are constants, specifically 6 and 10 respectively for this case.

A measure of the "goodness" of the equation is to calculate the sum of squares of the differences between observed and predicted (i.e., by the equation) values of the dependent variable. For example, for the first observation, the predicted value of y is $10 \times 3 + 6 = 36$, the observed value is 31, giving a difference of 5. The sum of squares of these values for each value of x is the quantity desired. Write a program to calculate this value for the above data.

5-7. An array of data consists of n experimental measurements of the variable x. Read them in and calculate their mean value and standard deviation:

$$\text{Mean value} = \frac{1}{n} \sum_{i=1}^{n} x_i = \bar{x}$$

$$\text{Standard deviation} = \sqrt{\frac{1}{n-1} \sum_{i=1}^{n} (x_i - \bar{x})^2}$$

Write out the mean value, the standard deviation, and n.

5-8. Redo Exercise 5-7 except in this exercise write out the value of x which is most different from the mean value of x.

5-9. A one-dimensional array **X** contains 20 elements which represent experimental measurements. These may be smoothed by calculating:

$$s.X_i = \frac{X_{i-1} + X_i + X_{i+1}}{3}$$

for all but the first and 20th elements. Read in X, calculate sX_i and write out the two arrays, one above the other.

†5-10. Five students take four examinations. Their marks are:

	Exam 1	Exam 2	Exam 3	Exam 4
Student 1	48.6	30.	62.8	23.4
Student 2	40.1	40.	60.1	29.6
Student 3	63.4	50.	63.7	31.2
Student 4	56.2	60.	58.2	27.3
Student 5	71.0	70.	67.3	26.4

Read in their marks as a table (a two-dimensional array). Calculate the average on each test, the average for each student on all four tests, and the average for all students on all tests.

5-11. Three construction men work a week (five days) and put in the hours shown:

	Day 1	Day 2	Day 3	Day 4	Day 5
Worker 1	8.0	8.5	9.5	8.0	8.5
Worker 2	8.0	8.5	10.0	8.0	9.0
Worker 3	8.0	9.0	9.0	9.0	8.5

Read in their hours as a table (a two-dimensional array). Calculate the total hours worked for each man, and the total hours worked by all men in the week.

5-12. One very useful item to a contractor on a construction project is the number of men of each craft required each week. Suppose he will need carpenters, plumbers, and electricians, hereafter referred to as crafts 1, 2, and 3, respectively. The contractor usually divides his total effort into various jobs which he then schedules to start on a given week. For each job, he estimates how many weeks are required and how many of each craft are needed. The information on each job is available via DATA statements containing the job number, the starting week, the weeks required, and the number of workers in crafts 1, 2, and 3.

Assuming the total duration of the contract is 10 weeks, write a program that determines the number of workers in each craft needed each week. The output should be in columnar fashion, with the week-number and the number of craftsmen needed in each craft. Use as input the following:

Job	Start	Duration	Craft 1	Craft 2	Craft 3
01	2	4	5	1	2
02	1	2	2	0	0
03	4	1	0	4	0

04	2	2	3	0	1
05	5	5	2	0	0
06	7	1	0	1	0
07	9	1	1	1	1

5-13. Read in a one-dimensional array **A** containing 8 elements. Sort the elements into an ascending order based on their absolute value, and write out the results.

5-14. Let $f(x) = a_n x^n + a_{n-1} x^{n-1} + \cdots + a_1 x + a_0$. A program is to be prepared to read n, read the coefficients of $f(x)$, read b and evaluate $f(b)$. The first entry is the value of n, the next $n + 1$ entries are the values of the coefficients (beginning with a_0), and the last entry is the value of b. Store the coefficients of $f(x)$ in a one-dimensional array.

Assume n will always be less than 50. Print b and $f(b)$.

As input, let $f(x) = -0.8x^5 - 0.06x^4 + 1.7x^3 - 3.2x^2 + 7x + 1$ and evaluate at $x = 0.75$. Although not the easiest to program, the most efficient manner to evaluate this polynomial is as follows:

$$((((-0.8x - 0.06) x + 1.7) x - 3.2) x + 7) x + 1$$

†5.15. Let $f(x) = a_n x^n + a_{n-1} x^{n-1} + \cdots + a_1 x + a_0$, let $g(x) = cx + d$, and let $h(x) = f(x)g(x) = b_{n+1} x^{n+1} + b_n x^n + \cdots + b_1 x + b_0$. Prepare a program to read n, c, and d, read the coefficients of $f(x)$ (beginning with a_0), calculate the coefficients of $h(x)$, and print the results. Use array **A** to store the coefficients of $f(x)$, and similarly for the coefficients of $h(x)$. The maximum value for n is 30.

As input, let $g(x) = 1.7x + 2.1$ and let $f(x) = x^5 + 1.6x^4 - 0.7x^3 + 0.2x^2 + 6.1x + 0.8$.

5-16. As a conscientious student in basket weaving, Joe Kollage has performed some bursting tests on his products. Since higher mathematics still baffle him, he would like you to write a program for him.

The experiment consisted of placing weights in each basket until it ruptured. Joe used three different weights—weight 1 weighing 5 pounds, weight 2, 10 pounds, and weight 3, 25 pounds. He performed this experiment on four baskets, and he has the number of weights of each type in the basket when it ruptured. The data for each test are entered in a separate **DATA** statement as follows:

	Number of Weight 1	Number of Weight 2	Number of Weight 3
Test 1	12	1	0
Test 2	6	2	1
Test 3	8	1	1
Test 4	0	2	2

Joe is confident he can keep the entries in order, so only the number of weights of each type for each test is entered. The program should proceed as follows:

1. Read input.
2. Calculate total weight in basket at rupture. This value should be stored in an array.
3. Calculate average weight at rupture.
4. Calculate the difference between individual test value and average test value.
5. Print test number, total weight at rupture, and difference from average for each test.
6. Print average weight at rupture.

This can be accomplished with only two loops.

5-17. Joe Bleaux needs to borrow $1,500 for a period of three years. After consulting three loan departments, he has the following possibilities:

1. 8% per year, compounded monthly
2. 8½ per year, compounded annually
3. 8¼% per year, compounded quarterly

Which one is the most attractive?

Write a program to calculate this. Read i, the annual interest rate, and m, the number of compounding periods annually. The final amount owed is $\$1,500 \cdot (1 + i/m)^{3m}$. The output should be the annual interest rate, the number of compounding periods annually, and the amount owed after three years. The output should be ordered so that the most attractive appears first and the least attractive last. Assume that the data are *not* read in this order.

5-18. Suppose we have the coordinates of five points in the x,y plane, and would like to find the distance between the two points that lie the farthest apart. The five points are:

x	y
-0.94	-3.22
-4.02	8.17
7.07	-9.11
5.49	8.76
0.20	4.45

The distance between the first two points is $\sqrt{(x_1 - x_2)^2 + (y_1 - y_2)^2}$; between the first and third is $\sqrt{(x_1 - x_3)^2 + (y_1 - y_3)^2}$; etc. Only the value of the farthest distance is to be printed. Be sure to check all possibilities (a total of 10).

5-19. Suppose we have an item of equipment worth $1,000 which we would like to depreciate over a five-year lifetime. We propose to do this via one of two ways:

1. Double-declining-balance method, where the depreciation for the year is $2/n$ times the book value at the beginning of the year (n = number of years over which item is to be depreciated).

2. Straight-line method, where the depreciation is $1/n$ times the original value of the equipment.

Write a computer program to calculate the depreciation by each of these methods and print a table, similar to the following:

Year	Double-Declining-Balance Depreciation	Year-End Book Value	Straight-Line Depreciation	Year-End Book Value
1	$400.00	$600.00	$200.00	$800.00
2	$240.00	$360.00	$200.00	$600.00
3	$144.00	$216.00	$200.00	$400.00
4	$ 86.40	$129.00	$200.00	$200.00
5	$ 51.84	$ 77.76	$200.00	$ 0.00

5-20. As can be seen from the table accompanying the previous problem, the double-declining balance depreciates equipment at a faster initial rate than does the straight-line method ($400 vs. $200, or twice as fast). However, this method will never reduce the book value to zero, since the depreciation is always a fraction of the present book value. This can be circumvented by using the double-declining-balance method during the initial years, and switching to the straight-line method at a later date. In fact, the switch should be made whenever the depreciation via the straight-line method would exceed that from the double-declining-balance method.

Write a program that depreciates a given amount over a given number of years (both read as inputs) via the above method. The output should appear as follows for depreciating $1,000 over a five-year period:

Year	Depreciation	Beginning Book Value
1	$400.00	$1,000.00
2	$240.00	$ 800.00
3	$144.00	$ 360.00
4*	$108.00	$ 216.00
5	$108.00	$ 108.00

*Switched to straight-line method.

†5-21. Let $f(x)$ be defined by the following equation:

$$f(x) = x^2 \sin(\pi x)$$

Prepare a program to perform the following functions:
1. Compute $f(x)$ at values of x at $0, 0.1, 0.2, \ldots, 1.0$.
2. Locate the maximum of these values.
3. Divide each of the above values by the maximum value to obtain normalized values.
4. Print as shown in the figure.

```
F(X) = X↑2 * SIN(3.1416*X)

X              F(X)              NOR F(X)
0              0                 0
0.1            3.09E-03          7.8E-03
0.2            0.02351           0.05931
0.3            0.07281           0.18367
0.4            0.15217           0.38386
0.5            0.25              0.63065
0.6            0.34238           0.86369
0.7            0.39642           1
0.8            0.37618           0.94895
0.9            0.2503            0.6314
1             -7.34639E-06      -1.8532E-05
```

Exercise 5-21.

5-22. Financial analysts take into account the time value of money via the net present value. To illustrate this concept, suppose an investment is expected to yield the returns given in the second column of the following table:

Year	Return	Present Value		
1	$7,000	$7,000/1.08$	=	6,481
2	9,000	$9,000/(1.08)^2$	=	7,716
3	13,000	$13,000/(1.08)^3$	=	10,320
4	20,000	$20,000/(1.08)^4$	=	14,701
5	40,000	$40,000/(1.08)^5$	=	27,233
		Net Present Value	=	66,441

The present value of the return is the amount that would have to be invested now to yield this return, as illustrated in the above table for an interest rate of 8%.

Write a program to calculate the net present value of the above investment for interest rates of 8%, 12%, and 15%. Store the returns in an array.

5-23. Suppose an initial investment of $60,000 yielded the returns given in the previous exercise. The discounted cash flow is the interest rate that will give a net present value of $60,000 as calculated by the procedure in the above exercise. This is a trial-and-error calculation. Suppose we assume the answer lies between an interest rate of 0% and 100%. Use the interval halving method in Exercise 4-11 to solve this problem. The plot of the net present value (NPV) will appear as follows:

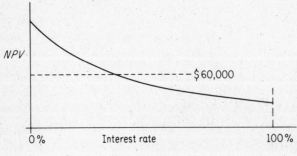

Exercise 5-23.

INPUT/OUTPUT

The simple basic forms of the **READ** and **PRINT** statements as presented in Chapter 2 are especially attractive to the beginning programmer, since they automatically provide the format for the information being transmitted. However, the advanced programmer may want to take advantage of some advanced features of BASIC to obtain formats more to his liking. It is the purpose of this chapter to present these topics.

6-1. Commas and Semicolons in PRINT Statements

As discussed in Chapter 2, the teletype line is normally divided into five zones of fifteen characters each. A comma causes the typer to move to the next print zone, or if the fifth print zone has been filled, to move to the first print zone of the next line (i.e., a carriage return).

If a comma follows the last variable in a **PRINT** statement, the carriage return is deleted. That is, using the statements

```
100   PRINT   A,
110   PRINT   B
```

causes **A** and **B** to appear on the same line. This feature is quite useful with **PRINT** statements appearing in loops, permitting values computed during each iteration of the loop to be printed on the same line. This is illustrated in the second type of output in Fig. 6-1. Note the use of two **PRINT** statements following the loop ending with line 90. The effect of the statement

```
100   PRINT
```

is to obtain a carriage return. Since the prior **PRINT** statement ended with a comma, this does not create a blank line in the output. The next statement

```
110   PRINT
```

generates another carriage return, and thus a blank line.

Use of a semicolon instead of a comma in **PRINT** statements results in shorter zones or "packed format." Instead of the regular fifteen spaces per zone, the spacing is typically as follows:

Digits in Number	Spaces in Zone
1,2,3	6
4,5,6	9
7,8,9	12

However, this varies from system to system, with some abandoning the zone concept entirely. In these systems, either two or three blank spaces follow the last character printed in order to allow the next output to begin on an even-numbered column. The last output in Fig. 6-1 illustrates the use of semicolons in PRINT statements.

```
LIST

MAR 25 21:16

10 PRINT "CARRIAGE RETURN"
20 FOR J=1 TO 4
30 PRINT J
40 NEXT J
50 PRINT
60 PRINT "NO CARRIAGE RETURN"
70 FOR J=1 TO 4
80 PRINT J,
90 NEXT J
100 PRINT
110 PRINT
120 PRINT "PACKED FORMAT"
130 FOR J=1 TO 4
140 PRINT J;
150 NEXT J
99999 END

> RUN
CARRIAGE RETURN
 1
 2
 3
 4

NO CARRIAGE RETURN
 1              2              3              4

PACKED FORMAT
 1  2  3  4
```

Fig. 6-1. Use of commas and semicolons in
PRINT statements.

As another example of the use of commas and semicolons in PRINT statements, consider the program in Fig. 6-2 that simply reads table T and prints it. In the output section, the PRINT statement in the inner loop ends with a comma, which allows us to place all elements in the same row on one line. The PRINT statement (line 120) in the outer loop produces a carriage return after printing each row. Use of a semicolon in line 100 would produce packed format.

A PRINT statement followed by a comma or semicolon can also be used in conjunction with the INPUT statement. For example, the statements

```
20  PRINT  "THE VALUE OF A IS",
30  INPUT  A
```

produce the output

```
THE VALUE OF A IS?
```

```
LIST

MAR 25 21:19

10 REM READ TABLE
20 FOR J=1 TO 5
30 FOR K=1 TO 3
40 READ T(J,K)
50 NEXT K
60 NEXT J
70 REM PRINT TABLE
80 FOR J=1 TO 5
90 FOR K=1 TO 3
100 PRINT T(J,K),
110 NEXT K
120 PRINT
130 NEXT J
140 DATA 1.31,-1.17,4.23
150 DATA 2.06,-0.11,0.45
160 DATA -1.17,2.10,1.97
170 DATA -2.01,5.09,0.88
180 DATA 0.02,1.25,-1.78
99999 END

> RUN
   1.31            -1.17            4.23
   2.06            -0.11            0.45
  -1.17             2.1             1.97
  -2.01             5.09            0.88
   0.02             1.25           -1.78
```

Fig. 6-2. Printing a table.

and **A** is entered on the same line. If the trailing comma is omitted from the **PRINT** statement, the output is

THE VALUE OF A IS
?

and **A** is entered on the line following the printed message. A semicolon following an alphanumeric string causes the succeeding input or output to begin in the very next column.

6-2. Output of Numerical Values

Although there are minor variations from one system to the next, the following general rules apply to the output of numerical values:

1. Numbers are left-justified in the zones, i.e., printing begins in the leftmost column.
2. Positive numbers are preceded by a blank space; negative numbers are preceded by the minus sign.
3. No decimal point accompanies integer numbers.
4. Trailing zeros following the decimal point are not printed.
5. Only six significant figures are printed for decimal notation.
6. The **E**-notation on output consists of the following:
    (a) A leading digit
    (b) A decimal point
    (c) Five trailing digits
    (d) The letter **E** followed by an integer number (sign plus two digits)

7. For integer numbers with more than nine digits (i.e., $\geq 10^9$), the **E**-notation is used.

8. If the decimal number is in the range of 0.1 to 10^6, the five or six most significant digits are printed without an exponent.

9. If, after deleting the trailing zeros on numbers less than 0.1, more than five digits remain, the number is printed in **E**-notation. That is, the number **8.278E-2** would be printed as **.08278**.

Virtually every system provides some means for altering the standard convention. Unfortunately, the features that accomplish this are by no means standard from one system to the next. Although several different approaches are outlined in the following paragraphs, the user must check to see which ones are supported on his system.

TAB. Perhaps the more common feature supported on most systems is the use of the **TAB** function. The general format of the function is

$$\text{TAB}\,(expression)$$

The *expression* is evaluated, the integer part is taken, and the result used to position the typer. This function appears in the **PRINT** statement along with the values to be printed. For example, the statement

$$\text{PRINT}\quad \text{A;TAB(20),B;TAB(40),C}$$

causes printing of **A** to begin in column 1, **B** to begin in column 20, and **C** to begin in column 40. The **TAB** function cannot be used to backspace the typer. If the typer has already passed the position specified by the argument in the **TAB** function, it is ignored completely. When using the **TAB** feature, the effect of commas and semicolons in the **PRINT** statement is unchanged. Since the use of semicolons minimizes the field widths, they should generally precede the **TAB** function. Some systems require that a semicolon follow the **TAB** function, while others permit either a comma or a semicolon. It has no effect on the spacing.

SETDIGITS. This feature provides the capability of specifying within the program the number of digits that will appear in the numerical output. The format of the statement is

$$\text{SETDIGITS}\,(expression)$$

The value of the *expression* (truncated to its integer value) represents the number of digits to appear in all numeric output in **PRINT** statements executed subsequent to executing the **SETDIGITS** statement. This value is not altered until another **SETDIGITS** statement is executed.

The integer part of the argument in the **SETDIGITS** statement must be between 1 and 11, inclusive. The sign of the number is printed in addition to the digits. If the integer part of the number cannot be contained in the specified number of digits, **E**-notation is used on output.

Figure 6-3 illustrates the effect of the **SETDIGITS** statement. Note rounding in the printed output.

PRINTUSING. Detailed specification of output can be obtained with the **PRINTUSING** statement and its associated Image statement, provided these features

```
LIST

MAR 25 21:15

10 FOR J=1 TO 11
20 SET DIGITS (J)
30 PRINT 9000/11
40 NEXT J
99999 END

> RUN
 8E+02
 8.2E+02
 818
 818.2
 818.18
 818.182
 818.1818
 818.18182
 818.181818
 818.1818182
 818.18181818
```

Fig. 6-3. Effect of the
SETDIGITS statement.

are implemented on the system. The format of the **PRINTUSING** statement is

PRINTUSING *n, output list*

where *n* is the line number of the associated Image statement and the *output list* contains the variables and alphanumeric information to be printed. The format of the associated Image statement is

n : *character string and conversion specifications*

The colon following the line number *n* designates this as an Image statement.

For example, the statements

```
180   LET   X=3
190   PRINTUSING   200,X,SQR(X)
200   :   THE SQUARE ROOT OF ##.## IS ##.##
```

give the output

THE SQUARE ROOT OF 3.00 IS 1.73.

The characters in the Image statement are reproduced on the output line with the values from the **PRINTUSING** statement edited into the spaces designated by the # characters.

The #'s may be collected into three types of groupings to form conversion specifications. These three are:

1. Integer or **I**-format specification, which consists of one or more # characters without an imbedded decimal. An example would be ####.

2. Decimal or **F**-format specification, which consists of one or more # characters, a decimal point, and if desired, additional # characters. An example would be ##.###.

3. Exponential or **E**-format specification, which consists of one or more # characters, a decimal point, additional # characters if desired, and finally four ! characters. An example would be #.###!!!!. Four ! characters *must* be supplied, one for the character **E**, one for the sign, and two for the integer exponent.

The other characters in the Image statement may be whatever is desired, and are simply reproduced in the output.

Any of the conversion specifications may be preceded by an optional sign. These are treated as follows:

1. No sign provided. If the value of the number to be printed is negative, the minus sign appears prior to the first printed digit, which reduces the length of the conversion specification by one.

2. A plus sign is provided. If the value transmitted is positive, a plus sign is edited into the output. If the value is negative, a minus sign is edited into the output. An example would be $+\#.\#\#\#$.

3. A minus sign is provided. This is treated the same as if a plus sign is provided except that positive numbers are written without a sign. An example is $-\#.\#\#\#$.

The desired output representation of a number to be printed is accomplished as follows:

1. *Integer format.* The value is truncated to an integer.

2. *Decimal or* **F**-*format.* The value is written in decimal form, extending with zeros to comply with the designated conversion specification. The last digit is rounded.

3. *Exponential format.* The value is converted to a decimal number with one digit to the left of the decimal and the corresponding power of ten. The fraction is rounded or extended with zeros as necessary. The position of the decimal point within the # characters is ignored, i.e., the field $\#\#.\#\#!!!!$ is equivalent to $\#.\#\#\#!!!!$.

If the length of the field resulting from the conversion is less than the spaces provided, the characters are right-justified. If the length exceeds the space available, asterisks are inserted into the corresponding spaces in the output.

Alphanumeric information, for example, information enclosed in quotations in the **PRINTUSING** statement, may also be inserted into the print line, and replaces all elements (sign, #, !, and decimal point) of the conversion specification. The information is left justified, with the unused spaces being filled with blanks. If the number of characters transmitted exceeds the number of spaces provided, the last characters are truncated.

If the **PRINTUSING** statement contains more fields than conversion specifications in the Image statement, the Image statement is reused with output beginning on a new line. If the **PRINT** statement contains fewer fields than does the Image statement, output is discontinued at the first unused conversion specification.

6-3. The RESTORE Statement

In some programs it may be desirable to read the same information from the **DATA** statements at two or more different locations in the program. This is accomplished by using the **RESTORE** statement, which upon execution causes the data block pointer to be reinitialized to the first element of the first **DATA** statement.

Figure 5-2 illustrated a program to compute the average age of a group of students and the difference between each student's age and the average. This was accomplished by reading the students' ages into an array, computing the average, and subtracting from each element in the array to obtain the difference from average. Figure 6-4 presents a program that accomplishes the same result by using a RESTORE statement instead of an array. The elements of the DATA statements must be read twice, once in each of the loops of the program.

```
LIST

MAR 25 21:13

10 LET S=0
20 FOR J=1 TO 7
30 READ A
40 LET S=S+A
50 NEXT J
60 LET M=S/7
70 PRINT "THE AVERAGE IS "M
80 PRINT
90 PRINT "STUDENT","AGE","DIFF"
100 RESTORE
110 FOR J=1 TO 7
120 READ A
130 PRINT J,A,A-M
140 NEXT J
150 DATA 22,19,29,20,25,23,22
99999 END

> RUN
THE AVERAGE IS  22.8571

STUDENT         AGE         DIFF
  1             22          -0.85714
  2             19          -3.85714
  3             29           6.14286
  4             20          -2.85714
  5             25           2.14286
  6             23           0.14286
  7             22          -0.85714
```

Fig. 6-4. Use of the RESTORE statement.

In some cases the DATA statements may also contain additional information prior to the information that is to be reread. For example, suppose the number of students was also to be entered via the first element in the DATA statement in the program in Fig. 6-4. That is, the program becomes

```
5 READ N
10 LET S=0
20 FOR J=1 TO N
30 READ A
40 LET S=S+A
50 NEXT J
60 LET M=S/N
70 PRINT "THE AVERAGE IS "M
80 PRINT
90 PRINT "STUDENT","AGE","DIFF"
100 RESTORE
105 READ A
110 FOR J=1 TO N
120 READ A
130 PRINT J,A,A-M
140 NEXT J
150 DATA 7,22,19,29,20,25,23,22
99999 END
```

Since the RESTORE statement always returns to the first element of the DATA block, an extra READ statement in line 105 must be used to pass over the first entry of the DATA statement.

Some systems circumvent the superfluous READ statements by extending the RESTORE statement to the form

$$\text{RESTORE } n$$

where n is a valid line number of one of the DATA statements. The effect of executing this statement is to initialize the data block pointer to the first element in the DATA statement in line n. Using this feature, the superfluous READ statement in line 105 of the above example could be avoided as follows:

```
100 RESTORE 160
        •
        •
        •
150 DATA 7
160 DATA 22,19,29,20,25,23,22
99999 END
```

6-4. Alphanumeric Variables

Otherwise known as string variables, these variables conveniently handle alphanumeric data such as names or other identifying information. Simple (that is, nonsubscripted) alphanumeric variables are designated by a single letter of the alphabet followed by the $ character.‡ Examples include A$, G$, etc. Most systems allow the variable or "string" to contain up to fifteen characters, some going as high as eighteen, and some imposing no limit.

Alphanumeric variables may be defined by a LET statement, an INPUT statement, or a READ statement. For example, the alphanumeric variable A$ could be defined by the statement

```
10  LET  A$="STICK EM UP"
```

where "STICK EM UP" could be called an alphanumeric constant. The use of the READ and DATA statements to define alphanumeric variables will be illustrated shortly.

When blanks appear in an alphanumeric variable, they are treated like any other character, and must be included in the character count. For example, the alphanumeric constant "STICK EM UP" contains eleven (11) characters.

The LET statement may also be used to assign an alphanumeric variable the same value as another alphanumeric variable. For example, the statement

```
10  LET  A$=B$
```

is valid. However, the mathematical operations $+$, $-$, $*$, $/$, and $\uparrow$ cannot be used with alphanumeric variables. This essentially means that only a single alphanumeric variable or an alphanumeric constant may appear on the right side of the equal sign in a LET statement.

---

‡A few systems will accept names containing 2 digits, e.g., AE$.

Most BASIC systems permit only one-dimensional arrays of alphanumeric variables although a few will accept two-dimensional arrays. Unless altered by a DIM statement, the implied size of the array is ten. Alphanumeric variables may be mixed with regular lists and tables in the DIM statement; for example,

DIM   T(4,4),A$(15),B(20)

Figure 6-5 illustrates the use of alphanumeric variables to store the description of the stock items for the inventory program described in Sec. 5-4. Note the use

```
LIST

MAR 25 21:09

5 DIM A$(6)
10 REM READ INITIAL INVENTORY
20 FOR J=1 TO 6
30 READ S(J),Q(J),A$(J)
40 NEXT J
50 REM UPDATE INVENTORY FOR STOCK RECEIVED
60 READ S1,Q1
70 IF S1=0 THEN 130
80 FOR J=1 TO 6
90 IF S1<>S(J) THEN 110
100 LET Q(J)=Q(J)+Q1
110 NEXT J
120 GOTO60
130 REM UPDATE INVENTORY FOR STOCK SHIPPED
140 READ S1,Q1
150 IF S1=0 THEN 210
160 FOR J=1 TO 6
170 IF S1<>S(J) THEN 190
180 LET Q(J)=Q(J)-Q1
190 NEXT J
200 GOTO 140
210 REM WRITE FINAL INVENTORY
220 PRINT "STOCK NO.","DESCRIPTION","QUANTITY"
230 FOR J=1 TO 6
240 PRINT S(J),A$(J),Q(J)
250 NEXT J
260 DATA 1207,12,"GIMMICKS"
270 DATA 1049,1,"CURE-ALLS"
280 DATA 0907,5,"GUESS WHAT"
290 DATA 0412,0,"UNDEFINED"
300 DATA 1222,7,"LOVE BEADS"
310 DATA 0015,2,"WIGS"
320 DATA 0412,5,0015,3,1049,7,1222,5,0412,5,0015,2,0,0
330 DATA 1207,2,1049,3,1222,10,0015,4,0412,7,0,0
99999 END

> RUN
STOCK NO.       DESCRIPTION      QUANTITY
    1207        GIMMICKS            10
    1049        CURE-ALLS            5
     907        GUESS WHAT           5
     412        UNDEFINED            3
    1222        LOVE BEADS           2
      15        WIGS                 3
```

Fig. 6-5. Use of alphanumeric variables.

of the READ statement to obtain values for the alphanumeric variables from the DATA statements.

Also note from Fig. 6-5 that the alphanumeric variables are used along with regular variables in the PRINT statement. However, when a semicolon follows the alphanumeric variable, the following output begins in the very next column.

Alphanumeric variables and alphanumeric constants may also be compared in the IF-THEN statement. The bulk of the applications test for either equality or inequality, an example being

100   IF   A$="MONDAY"   THEN   200

Only one alphanumeric variable or alphanumeric constant is permitted on each side of the relational operator. Virtually all systems permit the use of the operators = and <>, with some permitting the others (<, >, <=, >=). These latter systems use a collating sequence in comparing alphanumeric information, typically in the following order:

$$b'()*+,-./0123456789:;<=>ABC...XYZ$$

where **b** represents the blank character.

6-5. Files

The typical computer system on which BASIC is run can store information for later use in one of two places. First, it may store information in core storage, which we have referred to in several places in this manual. Information can be stored in or retrieved from core storage very quickly, on the order of one microsecond (one millionth of a second). The computer compiles and executes only programs in core storage. However, core storage is expensive, and only those programs that are currently being processed are stored in core storage.

The second storage device commonly used is a disk or drum. These devices store programs on a magnetic-coated surface that rotates under a read/write head. These devices are much cheaper than core storage and can store vastly larger quantities of information. However, the time required to retrieve or store information on these devices is much longer than for core, being around 20 milliseconds (20/1000 sec) for the faster devices.

Information on disks or drums is stored in areas called *files*. A file may contain virtually anything—numerical data, alphanumeric information, a program, etc. As one disk or drum may contain several files, each file must be given a name in much the same manner as a program is given a name. Options are generally provided to specify a password, account number, or other additional information to prevent or restrict the use, either accidental or intentional, by other users. Most systems either require or provide the option for the user to specify the size of the file. If an attempt is made to insert more information into a file that is filled, an error message will be generated.

Files are created by the user from the terminal by communicating with the computer's operating system, not with the BASIC compiler. The operating system is a master or executive program which supervises the functions of the digital computer. Creation of files is only one of its many functions. Unfortunately, operating systems differ widely, so the programmer must consult manuals specific to his system to learn how to create files.

As we have pointed out, one use of a file is to store a program to be used later. Suppose the program is entered from the terminal in much the same manner as we have entered previous programs. We may debug it, or may wait till later. Via commands from the terminal, we can instruct the computer to store our program in whatever file we desire. When we return, we can instruct the computer to retrieve the program from the file and place it in our working area of core storage. From this point we can proceed as if we had just entered the program from the terminal. Retrieving the program from the file does not erase the contents of the file. However, storing a program into the file erases whatever was there previously. If we retrieve a program from a file and make changes in the program, we must store the resulting program in the file if we want them incorporated next time we use the program.

Another use of files is to store data to be used by a program. This requires special input/output statements, which will be discussed in the remainder of this section.

Up to this point we have discussed only two mechanisms for the input of data: (1) the **READ** and **DATA** statements, and (2) the **INPUT** statement. For output, we have only discussed the **PRINT** statement. Whenever the same data is to be used by two or more programs or if the output from one program is to be the input to another, use of files is far more attractive than any of these.

Unfortunately, the versions of BASIC for different systems seem to differ more in regard to the features pertaining to files than in any other respect. We shall consequently have to discuss in terms of generalities to some extent. Before using files, the BASIC manual written specifically for the system being used should be consulted.

The operations dealing with files on any system must somehow encompass the following operations:
1. Creating the file
2. Opening the file
3. Closing the file
4. Writing information into the file
5. Reading information from the file
6. Reinitializing the file

We shall discuss each of these separately, followed by an example illustrating the use of files.

Before use, a file must be "opened," which activates the file prior to data transmission. At this time, it must also be specified whether information is to be read from the file (i.e., designate the file as an input file) or information is to be written into the file (i.e., designate the file as an output file). Some systems use the **OPEN** statement, while others do not. For example, on the IBM system the **OPEN** statement takes the form

$$\text{OPEN} \quad u, f, \quad \text{INPUT}$$

or

$$\text{OPEN} \quad u, f, \quad \text{OUTPUT}$$

where u = a numerical constant, variable, or expression

f = an alphanumeric variable or constant

To use a file named **SUSAN**, the **OPEN** statement could be

$$\text{OPEN} \quad 5, \text{"SUSAN"}, \quad \text{INPUT}$$

Future references within the BASIC program to the file would use the number 5 rather than the name SUSAN. This file can only be used as an input file.

The GE system does not require an OPEN statement as such. Instead, the name of the file accompanies each input, output, or other reference to the file. The first input statement that references a given file causes that file to be "opened" for input. Similarly, the first output statement that references a given file causes that file to be "opened" for output.

Most systems limit the number of files that may be "open" or active at any one time to around four or five. Some systems limit the number of open files to one for input and one for output. If one program uses several files, it may be necessary to close or deactivate one file before the system will permit the opening of another. The format of the CLOSE statement is generally the word CLOSE followed by either the name or number of the file, depending upon the system. At program termination, all open files are automatically closed. Execution of a CLOSE statement for a file that is already closed is permissible, although no action results. When an output file is closed, an end-of-file designator is appended to the file. When this file is subsequently read, an "out of data" error message is generated upon encounter of the end-of-file designator.

The format of the statements to read from a file or to write into a file is generally analogous to that of the READ, PRINT, and INPUT statements described previously. In fact, the GE system utilizes a modified version of the INPUT and PRINT statements for this purpose. The modification is that the name of the file enclosed in colons follows the word INPUT or PRINT. For example, the statement

90   INPUT:CLS:A,B

reads values for A and B from the file named CLS. Similarly, the statement

100   PRINT:CLS:A,B

writes the values of A and B into file CLS.

For this same purpose, the IBM system would use the GET or PUT statements. To read values of A and B from file 5, the statement would be

90   GET   5:A,B

Similarly, to write the values of A and B into file 5, the statement would be

100   PUT   5:A,B

In some cases, it may be necessary to reread the data from a file. This could be accomplished by closing the file and reopening it. The next access to the file would be to the first element in the file. Alternatively, most systems provide a special command for this purpose. On the IBM system, it is the statement RESET followed by the number of the file, for example

90   RESET   5

On the GE system, it is RESTORE followed by the name of the file enclosed in colons, for example

90   RESTORE:CLS:

The GE system provides another statement, **SCRATCH** followed by the name of the file in colons, that erases the file as well as reinitializes the pointer.

As an example of the use of files, the inventory program presented in Fig. 6-5 is modified so that the initial inventory is obtained from a file and the final inventory (after updating) is written back on a file as well as being printed. Before this program is run the very first time, the inventory must be stored on the appropriate file. The program in Fig. 6-6 accomplishes this task. The system on which this

```
LIST

APR  9 21:36  /CLLS/


10 REM PREPARATION OF INITIAL FILE
20 OPEN/CLS/,OUTPUT
30 FOR J=1 TO 6
40 READ S,Q,A$
50 PRINT FILE S,Q,A$
60 NEXT J
70 DATA 1207,12,"GIMMICKS"
80 DATA 1049,1,"CURE-ALLS"
90 DATA 0907,5,"GUESS WHAT"
100 DATA 0412,0,"UNDEFINED"
110 DATA 1222,7,"LOVE BEADS"
120 DATA 0015,2,"WIGS"
99999 END

> RUN
```

Fig. 6-6. Preparation of initial
inventory file. (CLLS is the name
of this program.)

program was run uses still another variation of the statements pertaining to files. In the **OPEN** statement in line 20, the file **CLS** (name enclosed in slashes) is designated as the input file. The loop between lines 30 and 60 simply reads the information for each item in inventory and prints it onto the file. Since this system permits only one file to be open for output at a given time, the **PRINT FILE** statement in line 50 need not contain the name of the file or other designation.

The inventory updating program in Fig. 6-7 is virtually identical to the program in Fig. 6-5 except for the statements pertaining to files. In fact, the line numbers are the same for most statements. In line 15 the file **CLS** is opened for input. The loop from lines 20 to 40 reads the beginning inventory from **CLS** using the **INPUT FILE** statement in line 30. Lines 50 through 210 are identical to the program in Fig. 6-5. The **CLOSE INPUT** statement in line 214 closes file **CLS** for input. The next statement opens the file for output. The loop from line 230 through 250 writes the final inventory onto file **CLS** as well as printing it.

Of course, the use of files could be readily extended to cover the stock received and the stock shipped.

6-6. In Summary

The exercises that follow this chapter are designed to require considerable attention to input and output of information. The purpose of the illustrated output in the exercises is to provide general guidelines as to how the output should

```
LIST

APR  9 21:33  /CLSS/


5 DIM A$(6)
10 REM READ INITIAL INVENTORY
15 OPEN/CLS/,INPUT
20 FOR J=1 TO 6
30 INPUT FILE S(J),Q(J),A$(J)
40 NEXT J
50 REM UPDATE INVENTORY FOR STOCK RECEIVED
60 READ S1,Q1
70 IF S1=0 THEN 130
80 FOR J=1 TO 6
90 IF S1<>S(J) THEN 110
100 LET Q(J)=Q(J)+Q1
110 NEXT J
120 GOTO 60
130 REM UPDATE INVENTORY FOR STOCK RECEIVED
140 READ S1,Q1
150 IF S1=0 THEN 210
160 FOR J=1 TO 6
170 IF S1<>S(J) THEN 190
180 LET Q(J)=Q(J)-Q1
190 NEXT J
200 GOTO140
210 REM WRITE FINAL INVENTORY
214 CLOSE INPUT
215 OPEN/CLS/,OUTPUT
220 PRINT "STOCK NO.","DESCRIPTION","QUANTITY"
230 FOR J=1 TO 6
240 PRINT S(J),A$(J),Q(J)
245 PRINT FILE S(J),Q(J),A$(J)
250 NEXT J
320 DATA 0412,5,0015,3,1049,7,1222,5,0412,5,0015,2,0,0
330 DATA 1207,2,1049,3,1222,10,0015,4,0412,7,0,0
99999 END

> RUN
STOCK NO.        DESCRIPTION      QUANTITY
  1207           GIMMICKS           10
  1049           CURE-ALLS          5
   907           GUESS WHAT         5
   412           UNDEFINED          3
  1222           LOVE BEADS         2
    15           WIGS               3
```

Fig. 6-7. Program to update inventory file. (CLSS
is the name of this program.)

appear. It is not intended that detailed attention be given to counting spaces and
the like in order to exactly match the output given.

Exercises

6-1. Program Exercise 5-5 without using subscripted variables.

6-2. Use a RESTORE statement to program the least squares problem in Sec. 5-5
without using subscripted variables.

6-3. Modify the PRINT statements so that array S in the program in Fig. 5-6
is not needed.

6-4. Use a list of alphanumeric variables for the names of the months to program Exercise 3-9.

6-5. Modify the inventory program in Fig. 6-5 so that the output is in ascending
order with respect to the number of items in stock.

†6-6. Modify the program for Exercise 5-2 so that the output contains the user's name along with his charge number. Assume this particular center has only ten users, whose names and corresponding charge numbers are as follows:

John Anderson	70206
Frank Wilson	40709
Joe East	50200
Myron Johnson	40201
Jack Evers	40710
Henry Williams	70207
John Smith	80001
Michael Sand	50201
Ralph Blue	70208
Horace White	40711

Using the time cards given as data for Exercise 5-2, the output of the program should appear as follows:

```
USER              CHARGE NO        TIME USED        PER CENT
 FRANK WILSON      40709            6.03             26.6033
 JOE EAST          50200            5.2              22.7571
 MYRON JOHNSON     40201            3.11             13.6105
 HENRY WILLIAMS    70207            5.1              22.3195
 JOHN SMITH        80001            3.36             14.7046
```

Notice that the user's name is not printed if he did not use any time.

6-7. Prepare a program to perform the following:
(a) Read the number of students in a class.
(b) Read one quiz score for each student along with his name.
(c) Arrange the scores in descending order.
(d) Compute the average score.
(e) Write average grade, the number of students making above average, and the number of students making below average.

```
AVERAGE SCORE    78.2857

NUMBER ABOVE AVERAGE          4

NUMBER BELOW AVERAGE          3

SCORE          NAME
 99            ROBERTS
 91            STEPHENS
 87            JONES
 82            KILROY          MEDIAN
 71            LEVEQUE
 62            NO NAME
 56            JAMES
```

Exercise 6-7.

(f) List the scores in descending order along with names. Write MEDIAN by median grade.

An example is shown in the accompanying illustration. The maximum number of students is 50, and allow 15 characters for each name.

6-8. Modify the program for Exercise 6-6 so that the largest user is listed first, second largest next, etc.

6-9. The following timetable is given for train schedules:

Distance	City	Time, P.M.
0	Chicago	4:00
93	Niles	6:42
141	Kalamazoo	7:28
164	Battle Creek	7:53
210	Jackson	8:39
248	Ann Arbor	9:18
284	Detroit	10:00

Prepare a program to read the above information, calculate the remaining entries in the table shown in the figure, and print in a similar fashion.

TRAIN SCHEDULE

DISTANCE	CITY	TIME P. M.		TIME FROM LAST STOP MIN	ELAPSED TIME MIN
0	CHICAGO	4	0	0	0
93	NILES	6	42	162	162
141	KALAMAZOO	7	28	46	208
164	BATTLE CREEK	7	53	25	233
210	JACKSON	8	39	46	279
248	ANN ARBOR	9	18	39	318
284	DETROIT	10	0	42	360

Exercise 6-9.

6-10. Consider writing a program to update a student's grade point average. Suppose data on each student are available as follows:

1. Student's name (15 characters or less)
2. Number of credit hours taken prior to this semester, followed by the number of credit hours earned.
3. Number of quality points earned prior to this semester.
4. The number of hours for his first class followed by the grade.
5. The number of hours for his second class followed by the grade.
6. etc. End of data indicated by a negative course hour.

A typical set of input might appear as follows:

JOE KOLLAGE	65	62	181	3B	3C	1A	4B	5B
KILROY	71	65	145	3C	5D	3F	3C	
JOE BLEAUX	48	48	159	3A	3B	5A	4B	

Grade point ratios are computed on the 4-point system, i.e., 4 points for A,

3 points for B, 2 points for C, 1 point for D (hours are earned), and 0 points for F (hours are not earned).

   Write a computer program that reads these data and prints the student's name, the number of credit hours taken, the number of credit hours earned, and his quality point ratio at the end of the term. If his quality point ratio is less than 2.0, place an asterisk prior to his name, as illustrated in the accompanying figure for the above input.

```
                   HOURS            HOURS            POINT
   NAME            TAKEN            EARNED           RATIO
   JOE KOLLAGE     81               78               2.80247
 *KILROY           85               76               1.90588
   JOE BLEAUX      63               63               3.36508
```

Exercise 6-10.

†**6-11.** Exercise 4-6 entailed the calculation of the capital-recovery factor for given interest rates. Write a program whose output is the table shown in the accompanying figure.

```
                          CAPITAL RECOVERY FACTOR
   PERCENT        2         4         6         8        10
   YEAR          **        **        **        **        **
      1    *     1.02      1.04      1.06      1.08      1.1
      2    *     0.515     0.5302    0.5454    0.5608    0.5762
      3    *     0.3468    0.3603    0.3741    0.388     0.4021
      4    *     0.2626    0.2755    0.2886    0.3019    0.3155
      5    *     0.2122    0.2246    0.2374    0.2505    0.2638
      6    *     0.1785    0.1908    0.2034    0.2163    0.2296
      7    *     0.1545    0.1666    0.1791    0.1921    0.2054
      8    *     0.1365    0.1485    0.161     0.174     0.1874
      9    *     0.1225    0.1345    0.147     0.1601    0.1736
     10    *     0.1113    0.1233    0.1359    0.149     0.1627
     11    *     0.1022    0.1141    0.1268    0.1401    0.154
     12    *     0.0946    0.1066    0.1193    0.1327    0.1468
     13    *     0.0881    0.1001    0.113     0.1265    0.1408
     14    *     0.0826    0.0947    0.1076    0.1213    0.1357
     15    *     0.0778    0.0899    0.103     0.1168    0.1315
```

Exercise 6-11.

6-12. Consider writing a program to print bank statements. The first entries for each account are the customer's name (15 characters), the second line of his address (15 characters), the third line (15 characters), his account number, and the balance at the beginning of the month. Each succeeding entry is a transaction, consisting of the date (day, month, and year) and the amount of the transaction (negative transactions indicate a check). A zero transaction indicates the end of the data. Write a program to process these data and print a statement as shown in the accompanying figure. Note that if a check and a deposit are made on the same day, they are written on the same line. The service charge is computed as follows:

1. No charge if the minimum balance is $400.00 or more.
2. A charge of 60¢ plus 4¢ per check less 20¢ per $100.00 of the minimum balance when under $400.00.

```
                              THE PHANTOM
                              2022 DUNGEON WAY
                              OUT OF THIS WORLD

          ACCOUNT NUMBER  1107

          DATE              WITHDRAWAL      DEPOSIT        BALANCE
          **************************************************************
                                                          412.41
          3 / 7    / 44   7.07                            405.34
          3 / 9    / 44   12.41                           392.93
          3 / 9    / 44   45.12                           347.81
          3 / 15   / 44   57.21                           290.6
          3 / 19   / 44   107.49          32.52           215.63
          3 / 22   / 44                   12.12           227.75
          3 / 22   / 44                   47.19           274.94
          3 / 27   / 44   52.12                           222.82
          4 / 5    / 44                   202.17          424.99
                          0.47 SC                         424.52
```

Exercise 6-12.

6-13. In some cases it would be desirable for a program to accept an input such as temperature in either degrees Fahrenheit or degrees centigrade. Suppose the temperature is the first entry, followed by an alphanumeric variable that is either F or C to indicate Fahrenheit or centigrade. Prepare a program to read an entry, make any necessary conversions, and print the temperature (appropriately labeled DEG F and DEG C) in both units. If the alphanumeric variable is neither F nor C, print the words ERRONEOUS INPUT. The program should be able to process as many entries as provided. Degrees F and degrees C are related as follows:

$$°C = \frac{5}{9} (°F - 32)$$

Double-space the output. Use as input 39°C, 48°F, 137°C, and 122°F.

6-14. The table in the accompanying figure gives the density (specific gravity) of NaOH solutions at various concentrations and temperatures. Write a program that reads the entries in this table from DATA statements and prints the table as shown.

```
                         TEMPERATURE, DEG F

                    50       86      122      176      212

              *     *        *        *        *        *

          2   *   1.023    1.018    1.01    0.993    0.98

          6   *   1.068    1.061    1.052   1.035    1.022
    PER
         10   *   1.113    1.104    1.094   1.077    1.064
    CENT
         14   *   1.158    1.148    1.137   1.12     1.107
    NAOH
         18   *   1.202    1.192    1.181   1.162    1.149

         22   *   1.247    1.235    1.224   1.205    1.191

              (SOURCE - INT. CRIT. TABLES, VOL. III,
                 PAGE 79)
```

Exercise 6-14.

6-15. Prepare a program to read the four coefficients of the polynomial

$$1.217x^3 + 1.798x^2 - 4.102x + 9.17$$

and print in the following fashion:

```
( 1.217 ) X↑ 3  + ( 1.798 ) X↑ 2  + (-4.102 ) X + ( 9.17 )
```

†**6-16.** If the order of the polynomial is unknown beforehand, the arrangement in the above exercise is not convenient. Instead, the output could be more conveniently arranged as follows:

```
( 1.217 ) X↑ 3  +
( 1.798 ) X↑ 2  +
(-4.102 ) X     +
( 9.17 )
```

Prepare a program to read the degree (maximum will be 50) of the polynomial followed by the coefficients, one per card.

The program should be able to read the data for one polynomial, print the results, and return to the first **READ** statement for another polynomial.

Use this program to print the following polynomials:

$$1.712x + 1.000$$

$$5.917x^4 + 1.722x^3 - 1.001x^2 + 0.022x + 1.00$$

$$1.000x^2 + 1.222x - 1.710$$

6-17. One frequent use of the computer is to generate tables of unusual functions. Suppose that for one reason or another someone needed a table of values of the function

$$\frac{\ln(x)}{(1 + |\sin x|)^2}$$

over the range 1 to 3 in steps of 0.02. Prepare a computer program to arrange the output as shown. This is similar to the common $\log_{10}$ tables.

		0	0.02	0.04	0.06	0.08
****	***
1	*	0	5.8E-03	0.0113	0.0166	0.0217
1.1	*	0.0266	0.0314	0.036	0.0404	0.0447
1.2	*	0.0488	0.0529	0.0568	0.0606	0.0644
1.3	*	0.068	0.0716	0.0751	0.0786	0.082
1.4	*	0.0854	0.0887	0.0919	0.0952	0.0984
1.5	*	0.1016	0.1048	0.108	0.1112	0.1144
1.6	*	0.1176	0.1208	0.124	0.1272	0.1305
1.7	*	0.1338	0.1371	0.1405	0.1439	0.1473
1.8	*	0.1509	0.1544	0.1581	0.1618	0.1656
1.9	*	0.1694	0.1734	0.1774	0.1816	0.1358
2	*	0.1901	0.1946	0.1992	0.2039	0.2087
2.1	*	0.2137	0.2189	0.2242	0.2296	0.2352
2.2	*	0.2411	0.2471	0.2533	0.2597	0.2664
2.3	*	0.2733	0.2805	0.2879	0.2956	0.3036
2.4	*	0.3119	0.3205	0.3295	0.3388	0.3485
2.5	*	0.3586	0.3691	0.3801	0.3916	0.4035
2.6	*	0.416	0.4291	0.4427	0.457	0.4719
2.7	*	0.4875	0.5039	0.521	0.539	0.5579
2.8	*	0.5777	0.5986	0.6205	0.6435	0.6677
2.9	*	0.6933	0.7202	0.7486	0.7786	0.8102
3	*	0.8437	0.8791	0.9165	0.9562	0.9983

Exercise 6-17.

6-18. Let $f(x)$ be evaluated at equally spaced intervals of x. For convenience, denote $f(x_i)$ as f_i. The first forward difference Δf_i can be defined as

$$\Delta f_i = f_{i+1} - f_i$$

where h is the difference between successive values of x. The second difference $\Delta^2 f_i$ is defined as

$$\Delta^2 f_i = \Delta f_{i+1} - \Delta f_i$$

Higher-order differences can be computed similarly, i.e.,

$$\Delta^{k+1} f_i = \Delta^k f_{i+1} - \Delta^k f_i$$

FINITE DIFFERENCES

X	F(X)	DEL	DEL2	DEL3
1	4			
		2.9696		
1.2	6.9696		1.3504	
		4.32		0.3456
1.4	11.2896		1.696	
		6.016		0.384
1.6	17.3056		2.08	
		8.096		0.4224
1.8	25.4016		2.5024	
		10.5984		0.4608
2	36		2.9632	
		13.5616		0.4992
2.2	49.5616		3.4624	
		17.024		0.5376
2.4	66.5856		4	
		21.024		0.576
2.6	87.6096		4.576	
		25.6		
2.8	113.21			

>

Exercise 6-18.

Let $f(x) = (x^3 + x^2)(x + 1)$. Let $h = 0.2$ and evaluate this function for consecutive values of x, beginning with $x = 1.0$. Calculate the first, second, and third differences and print as shown. Use a 20 × 5 array to store x, f, and the differences.

6-19. Consider the following equations:

$$y = (x + 1)^{1.2}$$

$$z = \frac{x^2}{x + 2}$$

These equations are to be evaluated for values of x from 0.0 to 3.0 in increments of 0.2. As the resulting function is to be plotted in perspective, consider the three-coordinate set of axes x, y, and z shown in the drawing. Although the axes are really perpendicular, the drawing must be made in two dimensions. Thus the z-axis is drawn at some angle φ to the x-axis. Given x_i, y_i, and z_i, the coordinates of point i, an exact location is specified in respect to the x-, y-, and z-axes as illustrated. However, this cannot be plotted very conveniently.

The plot would be much easier to make "indirectly." That is, the

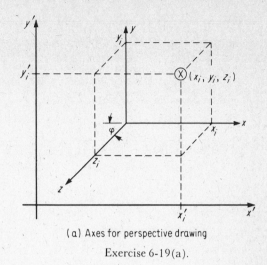

(a) Axes for perspective drawing

Exercise 6-19(a).

coordinates (x_i, y_i, z_i) are transformed into (x_i', y_i') for plotting on the two-dimensional coordinates superimposed in the drawing. The equations for these transformations are

$$y_i' = y_i - z_i \sin \varphi$$

$$x_i' = x_i - z_i \cos \varphi$$

Prepare a program to perform the following:
(a) Read the value of φ.
(b) Print φ and the (x_i', y_i') coordinates of points (4,0,0), (0,4,0), and (0,0,4), thus locating the extremities of the x-, y-, and z-axes.
(c) For the prescribed values of x, calculate y, z, x', and y'. The output should appear as shown. Let $\varphi = 35°$.

```
***** THREE-DIMENSIONAL PLOTTING *****

     PHI =   35 DEGREES

EXTREMITIES OF AXES          XP            YP

                X       4             0
                Y       0             4
                Z      -3.27671      -2.29416


X            Y             Z            XP            YP

0            1             0            0             1
0.2          1.24456       0.01818      0.18511       1.23414
0.4          1.49745       0.06667      0.34539       1.45922
0.6          1.7577        0.13846      0.48658       1.67828
0.8          2.02454       0.22357      0.61276       1.89345
1            2.2974        0.33333      0.72694       2.10622
1.2          2.57577       0.45         0.83137       2.31768
1.4          2.85926       0.57647      0.92777       2.52363
1.6          3.14752       0.71111      1.01747       2.73967
1.8          3.44025       0.85263      1.10154       2.95123
2            3.73719       1            1.18082       3.16365
2.2          4.03813       1.15238      1.256         3.37719
2.4          4.34285       1.30909      1.32762       3.59203
2.6          4.65118       1.46957      1.39616       3.80832
2.8          4.96295       1.63333      1.46201       4.02617
3            5.27803       1.8          1.52548       4.24566
```

(b) Output

Exercise 6-19(b).

Chapter 7

FUNCTIONS AND SUBROUTINES

Chapter 2 introduced several of the most commonly used functions available in BASIC. Appendix A gives a more complete list of the functions available on most BASIC systems. However, occasions arise when a function is needed that is not found in this list. In such situations the user may find it advantageous to define the needed function by using the DEF statement or to use a subroutine via the statements GOSUB and RETURN. This chapter discusses the use of these statements.

7-1. Definition of Functions

BASIC permits the user to define up to twenty-six functions via DEF statements. The name of all functions in BASIC contains three letters. The user-defined functions begin with the letters FN followed by a letter of the alphabet.

For example, suppose you are working a problem in which you frequently take the trigonometric sine of angles in degrees. Rather than convert from degrees to radians (i.e., divide by 57.3) at each point in the program, it may be more convenient to define a function, say FNS, that calculates the sine of an angle in degrees. The DEF statement to define this function could be

$$10 \quad \text{DEF FNS(X)} = \text{SIN(X/57.3)}$$

The DEF statements may appear anywhere in the program, but common practice is to place them early in the program. The expression following the equal sign may be any valid expression that can be coded onto one line of the program. Other functions (both intrinsic and user-defined) may be used in this expression.

The variable X, called the *argument*, enclosed in the parentheses of the function FNS in the DEF statement described in the previous example is a "dummy" variable. When the function FNS is "called," for example, by the statement

$$100 \quad \text{LET} \quad A = B * \text{FNS(T/2)}$$

the value of the expression T/2 is used in place of X in evaluating the function. The variable X may be used elsewhere in the program, and there is no connection between this variable and the "dummy" variable used in the DEF statement.

The DEF statement is also a nonexecutable statement. It only defines the function, execution occurring only when an expression containing the defined function is executed. From the **DEF** statement the compiler generates a block of code that may be executed. When the defined function appears in a statement elsewhere in the program, links are established with the block of code resulting from the **DEF** statement. Execution of the function is governed solely by where it is called from other statements, not by the position of the **DEF** statement in the program. This is why the **DEF** statement is said to be nonexecutable.

The defined function may contain variables other than the argument or "dummy" variable. For example, physical properties such as electrical resistance are frequently given as functions of such variables as temperature, an example being

$$R = a + bT + cT^2$$

This function can be defined by the statement

10   DEF FNR(T)=A+T*(B+C*T)

The variables **A**, **B**, and **C** are not "dummy" variables. Whenever the function **FNR** is evaluated, for example, by the statement

LET   V=I*FNR((T1+T2)/2)

the values of variables **A**, **B**, and **C** are used in evaluating the function. These variables must have been assigned values earlier in the program.

Some systems permit user-defined functions to have more than one argument. For example, if P dollars is invested at an interest rate i per compounding period for n compounding periods, the final worth of the investment would be $P(1 + i)^n$. The function $(1 + i)^n$ could be defined by the **DEF** statement

10   DEF FNA(I,N)=(1+I/100) ↑ N

where i is in percent. Note that the arguments are separated by commas, and are treated likewise in expressions using the function.

Suppose you wanted to compare investing money at 1/2 percent per month (compounded monthly) to investing at 6 1/2 percent (compounded annually). Figure 7-1 shows the results of investing $1,000 for 1 through 5 years. The function

```
LIST

APR  9 20:32

10 DEF FNA(I)=(1+I/100)↑N
20 PRINT "YEAR","1/2% PER MO","6.5% PER YR"
30 FOR J=1 TO 5
40 LET N=12*J
50 LET P=1000*FNA(.5)
60 LET N=J
70 PRINT J,P,1000*FNA(6.5)
80 NEXT J
99999 END

> RUN
YEAR           1/2% PER MO      6.5% PER YR
 1                1061.68          1065
 2                1127.16          1134.23
 3                1196.68          1207.95
 4                1270.49          1286.47
 5                1348.85          1370.09
```

Fig. 7-1. Use of user-defined function.

defined in line 10 is called *once in line 50* and *once in line 70*. In this function, I is a "dummy," but N is not.

Each defined function must have at least one argument, although it is not necessary that any or all of the arguments be used in the expression in the DEF statement. The arguments in the DEF statement must be distinct, but two or more may be identical in the calling statement. That is, the statement

$$10 \quad \text{DEF FNX(A,B,A)} = A \uparrow 2 + B \uparrow A$$

is rejected. However, the statement

$$\text{LET} \quad X = \text{FNY}(X,X)$$

is acceptable.

7-2. Subroutines

Whenever the same operations are called for in two or more different locations in a program, a subroutine can be used to provide these operations, thereby avoiding duplicate coding. Transfer to the subroutine is obtained via a GOSUB statement whose format is

$$\text{GOSUB } n$$

where n is the line number of the first statement in the subroutine. For example, the statement

$$100 \quad \text{GOSUB} \quad 460$$

instructs the computer to transfer control to line 460. This is virtually identical to the GOTO statement *except* that the computer remembers where it was when it transferred to line 460. Upon encounter of a RETURN statement, control is transferred back to the first statement following the GOSUB statement. The format of the return statement is simply

$$\text{RETURN}$$

It is *not* followed by a line number since the computer remembers the last GOSUB that was executed and simply transfers control to the line following the GOSUB statement.

It is thus possible to use GOSUB statements "calling" the same subroutine from several different locations in the same program. Since the computer remembers which GOSUB statement was executed last, no mixup occurs. This is illustrated by the following example.

As an illustration of the use of subroutines in BASIC, consider evaluation of the binomial coefficients $\binom{n}{j}$ which are given by the expression

$$\binom{n}{j} = \frac{n!}{j!\,(n - j!)}$$

where $n! = 1 \times 2 \times \cdots \times (n - 1) \times n$ and $0! = 1$. Suppose our program is to read n and j and evaluate the binomial coefficient. Note that this coefficient can be readily evaluated if the factorials can be calculated. The following statements calculate the factorial of **K**:

```
500 REM COMPUTATION OF F=K FACTORIAL
510 LET F=1
520 IF K=0 THEN 560
530 FOR L=1 TO K
540 LET F=F*L
550 NEXT L
560 RETURN
```

The entire program to calculate the binomial coefficient is shown in Fig. 7-2. Note the **GOSUB** statements in lines 40, 80, and 120 to calculate each of the factorials.

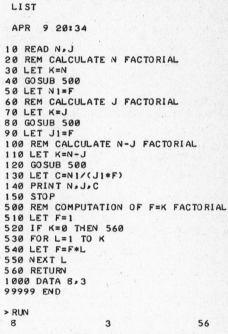

```
LIST

APR  9 20:34

10 READ N,J
20 REM CALCULATE N FACTORIAL
30 LET K=N
40 GOSUB 500
50 LET N1=F
60 REM CALCULATE J FACTORIAL
70 LET K=J
80 GOSUB 500
90 LET J1=F
100 REM CALCULATE N-J FACTORIAL
110 LET K=N-J
120 GOSUB 500
130 LET C=N1/(J1*F)
140 PRINT N,J,C
150 STOP
500 REM COMPUTATION OF F=K FACTORIAL
510 LET F=1
520 IF K=0 THEN 560
530 FOR L=1 TO K
540 LET F=F*L
550 NEXT L
560 RETURN
1000 DATA 8,3
99999 END

> RUN
8                3                56
```

Fig. 7-2. Use of **GOSUB** statement.

Also note the **STOP** statement in line 150 to prevent entry of the subroutine other than via a **GOSUB** statement.

Although tempting, it is not permissible to leave a subroutine other than via **RETURN** statement. There may, however, be more than one **RETURN** statement in the subroutine.

A single program may contain more than one subroutine. In fact, one subroutine may call another, giving "nested" **GOSUB**'s. In this case, more than one **GOSUB** statement will be executed prior to executing a **RETURN** statement, as illustrated in the following example.

The expansion of the expression $(x + a)^n$ is given by the following expression:

$$(x + a)^n = \sum_{j=0}^{n} \binom{n}{j} a^j x^{n-j}$$

where a is a constant and $\binom{n}{j}$ is the binomial coefficient calculated earlier.

To illustrate the use of "nested" subroutines, suppose we use the program in Fig. 7-2 as the starting point of a program to calculate the coefficients of the above polynomial. The final program is illustrated in Fig. 7-3. The program first

```
LIST

APR  9 20:58

10 READ A,N
20 PRINT "POWER OF X","COEFFICIENT"
30 FOR J=0 TO N
40 GOSUB 300
50 LET C1=C*A↑J
60 PRINT N-J,C1
70 NEXT J
80 STOP
300 REM COMPUTE BINOMIAL COEFFICIENT
310 LET K=N
320 GOSUB 500
330 LET N1=F
340 LET K=J
350 GOSUB 500
360 LET J1=F
370 LET K=N-J
380 GOSUB 500
390 LET C=N1/(J1*F)
400 RETURN
500 REM COMPUTATION OF F=K FACTORIAL
510 LET F=1
520 IF K=0 THEN 560
530 FOR L=1 TO K
540 LET F=F*L
550 NEXT L
560 RETURN
1000 DATA 2.6,8
99999 END

> RUN
POWER OF X         COEFFICIENT
   8               1
   7               20.8
   6               189.28
   5               984.256
   4               3198.83
   3               6653.57
   2               8649.64
   1               6425.45
   0               2088.27
```

Fig. 7-3. Use of nested GOSUB's.

reads values for A and N, and then prints the headings for the output. The loop from lines 30 to 70 computes each of the coefficients. The GOSUB in line 40 essentially calls the program in Fig. 7-2. Lines 300 to 400 in Fig. 7-3 are essentially identical to lines 30 through 150 of the program in Fig. 7-2, except that the REM and PRINT statements have been removed and the STOP statement has been replaced by a RETURN statement. Note that two GOSUB statements are executed before a RETURN statement is executed.

7-3. Summary

The user-defined function and subroutine features of BASIC can be utilized for a variety of purposes, one of which is to give a modular structure to a program. Furthermore, these proven modules may also be conveniently incorporated into other programs as the need arises.

Exercises

7-1. The logarithm to any base, say b, can be calculated by the equation

$$\log_b(x) = \ln(x)/\ln(b)$$

Using a user-defined function, compute

$$\log_2(25), \quad \log_4(17), \quad \text{and} \quad \log_{27}(19)$$

7-2. If the statement

LET   A   =   B↑ .3333

or similar version is used to compute the cube root of **B**, an error is likely to be generated if **B** is negative. This can be circumvented by programming as either

LET   A   =   ABS(B) ↑ 1.3333/B

or

LET   A   =   ABS(B) ↑ .3333*SGN(B)

Using a user-defined function, compute the cube roots of 7.26 and −1.79.

†7-3. The only inverse trigonometric function available in most versions of BASIC is the arctan. Prepare a user-defined function to compute the arcsin (in degrees), where

$$\arcsin(x) = \arctan(x/\sqrt{1 - x^2})$$

Assume $x < 1$. Compute the arcsin of 0.726.

7-4. If two sides of a right triangle are a and b, the hypotenuse is given by $\sqrt{a^2 + b^2}$. Prepare a user-defined function to compute this. Compute the hypotenuse if $a = 2$ and $b = 5$.

7-5. The hyperbolic sine is given by the equation

$$\sinh(x) = \frac{e^x - e^{-x}}{2}$$

Prepare a user-defined function to compute the hyperbolic sine. Compute the hyperbolic sine of 1.27. (*Note:* On many versions of BASIC, the hyperbolic sine is available as an intrinsic function.)

7-6. Use a user-defined function for $f(x)$ to program Exercise 4-11.

†7-7. The derivative $f'(x)$ of a function $f(x)$ at $x = a$ is approximately given by

$$f'(a) = \frac{f(a + h) - f(a)}{h}$$

for h small. Using a user-defined function, compute the derivative of

$$f(x) = 4x^3 - x^2 + \ln(x)/x$$

at $x = 4$. Run for $h = 0.001, 0.01,$ and 0.1.

7-8. Using a user-defined function for $f(x)$ and another user-defined function for $f'(x)$ via the technique presented in the previous example, program Exercise 4-12. Use $h = 0.01$.

7-9. Use a user-defined function for $f(x)$ in programming Exercise 4-14.

7-10. Use a user-defined function for $f(x)$ in programming Exercise 4-17.

7-11. Use a user-defined function for $f(x)$ in programming Exercise 4-19.

†7-12. By using a subroutine instead of a user-defined function, an "error message" can be incorporated into the routine calculating the arcsin for Exercise 7-3. If the magnitude of x is greater than one, the message

ARCSIN (value of x) DOES NOT EXIST

should be printed and execution terminated.

7-13. Program Exercise 3-26 using a subroutine to compute the arctangent and place in the proper quadrant.

7-14. Prepare a subroutine to arrange elements of an array in ascending order as discussed in Sec. 5-4. Use this subroutine to place both columns of the table

1	4
−2	3
4	9
7	2
−5	−1

in ascending order and print the final table.

7-15. Consider preparing a program to compute the greatest common divisor of three numbers. Suppose we pick two of the numbers and find their greatest common divisor. We can then take the result of this computation and the third number and find their greatest common divisor, which will be the greatest common divisor for all three.

A simple-minded approach to finding the greatest common divisor of two numbers is to try each number from 1 to the magnitude of the smallest of the two numbers. There are more efficient approaches, but this will suffice for our problem.

Using subroutines, write a program to find the greatest common divisor of the following numbers:

40, 80, 100
21, 41, 82
21, 42, 99

MAT STATEMENTS

A useful extension of BASIC is the inclusion of statements specifically designed to permit matrix computations. Although any or all of the capabilities available via these statements can be accomplished with the BASIC statements discussed in previous chapters, one of the statements designed for matrix computations can be used in the place of several regular BASIC statements. This makes the program shorter, easier to follow, less likely to contain errors, and easier to debug if it does.

We shall tacitly assume that the reader is familiar with terms such as matrix addition, matrix subtraction, matrix multiplication, matrix inversion, etc. Although it is realized that a number of readers may not fall into this category, discussion of matrix mathematics is omitted from this text because (1) a number of good works on this subject are available, and (2) the primary purpose of this text is to describe the features of BASIC.

8-1. Specification of Dimensions

As matrices are also two-dimensional arrays like tables, the rules for naming matrices are the same as for tables and lists as discussed in Chapter 5. That is, names are restricted to being only a single letter of the alphabet. When appearing in a DIM statement, the space reserved for the matrix is specified by the two integer numbers separated by a comma, the first number specifying the number of rows and the second specifying the number of columns. That is, the statement

10   DIM   A(3,5)

specifies that matrix A will have 3 rows and 5 columns.‡

Recall that the DIM statement only reserves the designated number of storage locations. As pointed out in Chapter 5, it is not necessary to use all of the reserved storage locations. You may use fewer, but never more. That is, we may read a 2 × 2 matrix into the array A specified by the above DIM statement.

---

‡The discussion in this chapter will, for the most part, assume that zero subscripts are not allowed, which seems to be the trend. However, programs using MAT statements that run on a system that does not use the zero subscript will *not* run on a system that does. The converse is also true. In the examples for this chapter, we shall present both versions. Some systems, notably the Dartmouth Time Sharing System BASIC, recognize the zero subscript in arrays but do not use the zero row or column in MAT operations.

The size of the matrix as utilized in the computations is specified by statements other than the DIM statement. This permits the dimensions of a matrix to be varied to meet the needs of the program, provided the storage locations set aside in the DIM statement are not exceeded. There are four statements which define the size of a matrix while at the same time serving another purpose. Three of these are discussed in this section, and the last one will be covered in the next section.

Zero. The statement

$$120 \quad MAT \quad A = ZER(2,3)$$

causes matrix A to be treated as having two rows and three columns (i.e., a 2×3 matrix), and is filled out with zeros. Subsequent references to matrix A also assume it is a 2×3 matrix unless its dimensions are redefined by another ZER statement or one of the other statements discussed below. If the size of the matrix is not to be changed, the dimensions may be deleted from the ZER statement. That is, if A was previously defined as being a 2×3 matrix, the statement

$$120 \quad MAT \quad A = ZER$$

serves the same function as the statement presented earlier. It is also permissible to use variables or expressions in the ZER statement to specify dimensions.

Constant. If the matrix A is to be filled out with ones instead of zeros, the statement

$$120 \quad MAT \quad A = CON(2,3)$$

is used. Otherwise, the CON statement is identical to the ZER statement.

Identity. If the matrix A is to be the identity matrix (i.e., ones on the diagonal and zeros elsewhere), the statement

$$120 \quad MAT \quad A = IDN(N,N)$$

is used. Since the matrix must be square (number of rows equals number of columns) in order for the identity matrix to be meaningful, some systems permit IDN to have only one argument, while others use only the first argument even if two are given.

8-2. Input-Output

The fourth type of statement that can define the size of a matrix is the MAT READ statement, an example being

$$100 \quad MAT \quad READ \quad A(2,3)$$

This statement defines A to be a 2×3 matrix and reads values for the elements row by row from the DATA statements. That is, the input sequence is A(1,1), A(1,2), A(1,3), A(2,1), A(2,2), and A(2,3). This one statement is equivalent to the nested loops

```
100 FOR J=1 TO 2
110 FOR K=1 TO 3
```

```
120 READ A(J,K)
130 NEXT K
140 NEXT J
```

It is also possible to read the dimensions of the matrix from the **DATA** statements. An example of this is

```
10 DIM A(15,15)
100 READ J,K
110 MAT READ A(J,K)
```

where **J** and **K** are less than or equal to 15. Note that **J** and **K** cannot be read with the **MAT READ** statement. It is, however, permissible to read two or more matrices with the same **MAT READ** statement.

The **MAT INPUT** statement is analogous to the **MAT READ** statement except that input is via the teletype.

Output is via the **MAT PRINT** statement, which prints the matrix row-by-row using the dimensions assigned previously. Blank lines are always inserted between rows. Examples of this statement include

```
100 MAT PRINT A
110 MAT PRINT B;
120 MAT PRINT A;B
```

In the first example the elements of **A** are written row-by-row with five elements per line. The second example is analogous to the first except that packed format will be used. The last example causes packed format to be used for **A** and regular format for **B**. Commas following the last matrix in the **MAT PRINT** statement have no effect. That is, the statement

```
100 MAT PRINT A,
```

is equivalent to

```
100 MAT PRINT A
```

A semicolon following the last matrix in the **MAT PRINT** statement results in packed format.

8-3. Arithmetic Operations with Matrices

Virtually all systems perform matrix addition, subtraction, multiplication (scalar and matrix), transposition, and inversion. In all of these operations, it is generally necessary that the size of the matrix on the left of the equal sign has been previously defined by either a **ZER**, **CON**, **IDN**, **MAT READ**, or similar statement. That is, many systems do not automatically size the matrices, although some later systems have incorporated this feature.

Addition. Matrix addition is obtained by statements of the type

```
100 MAT A=B+C
```

which causes the elements of **C** to be added to the respective elements of **B** to give the respective elements of **A**. For this operation to be meaningful, the dimensions of matrices A, B, and C must be identical. It is permissible for the same matrix to appear on both sides of the equal sign, for example,

$$100 \quad \text{MAT} \quad \text{A=B+A}$$

However, only one operation can be specified on the right of the equal sign. Consequently, the statement

$$100 \quad \text{MAT} \quad \text{A=B+C+D}$$

will not be accepted. Nor can the MAT statement be used to add a matrix to part of another matrix.

Subtraction. Subtraction of one matrix from another is obtained by statements such as

$$100 \quad \text{MAT} \quad \text{A=B-C}$$

The rules governing this statement are identical to those governing the matrix add statement.

Scalar Multiplication. The statement

$$100 \quad \text{MAT} \quad \text{A=(expr)*B}$$

causes each element in B to be multiplied by the scalar value of the expression. The parentheses are required because BASIC permits a scalar and a matrix to have the same name. Examples include:

```
 90 MAT B=(2)*A
100 MAT A=(2)*A
110 MAT G=(2*SQR(K)-5)*C
120 MAT X=(1)*Y
```

Note that the scalar portion is always enclosed in parentheses. As illustrated by the second example, the same matrix may appear on both sides of the equal sign. The last example essentially copies matrix Y into matrix X. On some systems, this type of statement must be used for this purpose since the statement

$$120 \quad \text{MAT} \quad \text{X=Y}$$

would not be recognized.

Matrix Multiplication. The statement for matrix multiplication is

$$90 \quad \text{MAT} \quad \text{C=A*B}$$

This operation is defined only if

    (a) The number of columns in A equals the number of rows in B.
    (b) The number of rows in C equals the number of rows in A.
    (c) The number of columns in C equals the number of columns in B.

If any one of these is not satisfied, an error message is generated. For this statement the same variable may *not* appear on both sides of the equal sign.

Transpose. The transpose of matrix A is copied into matrix B by the statement

$$100 \quad \text{MAT} \quad \text{B=TRN(A)}$$

If the size of A is $n \times m$, the size of B must be $m \times n$. In-place transposition is not allowed. That is the statement

$$100 \quad \text{MAT} \quad A = \text{TRN}(A)$$

is not accepted.

Inversion. Matrix inversion is obtained by statements of the type

$$100 \quad \text{MAT} \quad A = \text{INV}(B)$$

where **A** and **B** are square matrices of the same size. If matrix **B** is singular, an error is generated. Matrix inversion in-place, for example,

$$100 \quad \text{MAT} \quad A = \text{INV}(A)$$

is not allowed. (*Caution:* some systems destroy the matrix used as the argument of the **INV** function.)

8-4. Vectors

Single dimensional arrays or lists may be used as vectors in the **MAT** statements. A vector is really a matrix with only one row (a row-vector) or one column (a column vector). For example, suppose the one-dimensional array **P** is dimensioned by the statement

$$10 \quad \text{DIM} \quad P(20)$$

This vector may be treated as a row vector if entered by the **READ** statement

$$20 \quad \text{MAT} \quad \text{READ} \quad P(1,5)$$

Alternatively, it would be treated as a column vector if read by the statement

$$20 \quad \text{MAT} \quad \text{READ} \quad P(5,1)$$

The selection of which of these to use is governed by the way the vector will be used in subsequent **MAT** statements.

8-5. Examples

A theorem in linear algebra states that if matrices **A** and **B** are square, are of the same order, and are nonsingular, the following relationship holds:

$$(\mathbf{AB})^{-1} = \mathbf{B}^{-1}\mathbf{A}^{-1}$$

Consider preparation of a program to compute and print both sides of the equation for the matrices

$$\mathbf{A} = \begin{bmatrix} 1 & 2 & 1 \\ 3 & 7 & 2 \\ 1 & 0 & 1 \end{bmatrix}$$

$$\mathbf{B} = \begin{bmatrix} 2 & 0 & 4 \\ 1 & 0 & 7 \\ 1 & 2 & 1 \end{bmatrix}$$

The resulting program is shown in Fig. 8-1, one version for systems that do not recognize zero subscripts and one version for systems that do.

```
LIST

APR 9 20:54

10 DIM A(5,5),B(5,5),C(5,5),D(5,5)
20 MAT READ A(3,3),B(3,3)
30 MAT C=ZER(3,3)
40 MAT D=ZER(3,3)
50 MAT C=A*B
60 MAT D=INV(C)
70 PRINT "A*B INVERSE"
80 MAT PRINT D
90 MAT C=INV(B)
100 MAT D=INV(A)
110 MAT A=C*D
120 PRINT "B INVERSE*A INVERSE"
130 MAT PRINT A
140 DATA 1,2,1,3,7,2,1,0,1
150 DATA 2,0,4,1,0,7,1,2,1
99999 END
```

(a) Program for systems not recognizing zero
    subscripts (output shown in b)

```
LIST

APR 9 20:51

10 DIM A(5,5),B(5,5),C(5,5),D(5,5)
20 MAT READ A(2,2),B(2,2)
30 MAT C=ZER(2,2)
40 MAT D=ZER(2,2)
50 MAT C=A*B
60 MAT D=INV(C)
70 PRINT "A*B INVERSE"
80 MAT PRINT D
90 MAT C=INV(B)
100 MAT D=INV(A)
110 MAT A=C*D
120 PRINT "B INVERSE*A INVERSE"
130 MAT PRINT A
140 DATA 1,2,1,3,7,2,1,0,1
150 DATA 2,0,4,1,0,7,1,2,1
99999 END
```

```
> RUN
A*B INVERSE
-2.65            0.7            1.25

 2.85           -0.8           -0.75

 0.45           -0.1           -0.25


B INVERSE*A INVERSE
-2.65            0.7            1.25

 2.85           -0.8           -0.75

 0.45           -0.1           -0.25
```

(b) Programs for systems that recognize
    zero subscripts

Fig. 8-1. Illustration of MAT
statements.

The DIM statement in line 10 reserves storage for four 5×5 matrices A, B, C, and D. The READ statement in line 20 reads A and B and defines them to be 3×3 matrices. In lines 30 and 40 the ZER function is used to define the sizes of C and D to be 3×3 also. Lines 50 and 60 compute $(A*B)^{-1}$, which is printed in line 80. Lines 90, 100, and 110 compute $B^{-1}*A^{-1}$, which is stored in A since the original matrix is no longer needed. Line 130 prints the result.

The MAT statements can also be conveniently used to compute the solution to simultaneous equations. For example, the simultaneous equations

$$3x_1 + 4x_2 - x_3 = 0$$
$$2x_1 + 7x_2 + x_3 = 9$$
$$x_1 - 2x_2 - 4x_3 = -2$$

can be written in matrix form as follows:

$$\begin{bmatrix} 3 & 4 & -1 \\ 2 & 7 & 1 \\ 1 & -2 & -4 \end{bmatrix} \begin{bmatrix} x_1 \\ x_2 \\ x_3 \end{bmatrix} = \begin{bmatrix} 0 \\ 9 \\ -2 \end{bmatrix}$$

or

$$\mathbf{Ax} = \mathbf{b}$$

The solution is given by

$$\mathbf{x} = \mathbf{A}^{-1}\mathbf{b}$$

provided matrix **A** is nonsingular.

The program in Fig. 8-2 computes the solution. Note that **x** and **b** are defined as one-dimensional arrays in the DIM statement, and are dimensioned as column vectors in lines 20 and 40.

Actually, this example does not constitue an efficient method for solving a set of simultaneous equations. Virtually any math text will point out that such equations can generally be solved by methods much more efficient than the one above.

8-6. Extensions

The prior discussions in this chapter have presented the MAT statements common to most all systems. The features described below are found on some systems, but the user should investigate these further before using them.

Copy. Many of the more recent versions of BASIC accept the statement

$$\text{MAT} \quad A = B$$

which simply copies matrix B into matrix A.

Dimensioning. Some systems also incorporate one or more of the following features:

(a) The size of the matrix specified in the DIM statement is used as the dimension of the matrix until redefined in a CON, ZER, IDN, MAT READ,

```
LIST

APR  9 20:46

10 DIM X(3),A(3,3),B(3),C(3,3)
20 MAT READ A(3,3),B(3,1)
30 MAT C=ZER(3,3)
40 MAT X=ZER(3,1)
50 MAT C=INV(A)
60 MAT X=C*B
70 MAT PRINT X
80 DATA 3,4,-1,2,7,1,1,-2,-4
90 DATA 0,9,-2
99999 END
```

(a) Program for systems that do not recognize
    zero subscripts (output shown in b)

```
LIST

APR  9 20:44

10 DIM X(3),A(3,3),B(3),C(3,3)
20 MAT READ A(2,2),B(2,0)
30 MAT C=ZER(2,2)
40 MAT X=ZER(2,0)
50 MAT C=INV(A)
60 MAT X=C*B
70 MAT PRINT X
80 DATA 3,4,-1,2,7,1,1,-2,-4
90 DATA 0,9,-2
99999 END

> RUN
-4.51613

 2.87097

-2.06452
```

(b) Program for systems that recognize zero
    subscripts

Fig. 8-2. Program for solving simultaneous equations.

or similar statement. Thus the statement

$$10 \quad DIM \quad A(2,3)$$
$$20 \quad MAT \quad READ \quad A$$

would cause six elements to be read and stored in A.

(b) Some systems automatically assign the proper dimensions to the variable
     on the left of the equal sign. Such systems would process statements
     such as

$$10 \quad DIM \quad A(10,10),B(10,10),C(10,10)$$
$$20 \quad MAT \quad READ \quad A(2,3),B(3,3)$$
$$30 \quad MAT \quad C=A*B$$

The dimensions of C would be 2×3 following line 30.

(c) Some systems also accept statements that simply define the size of the
     matrices. For example, the statements

$$10 \quad DIM \quad A(10,10)$$
$$20 \quad MAT \quad SIZE \quad A(2,3)$$
$$30 \quad MAT \quad READ \quad A$$

are equivalent to

```
10   DIM   A(10,10)
20   MAT   READ   A(2,3)
```

Determinant. On many recent systems, the function INV evaluates the determinant of the argument matrix as well as its inverse. This feature varies from system to system. One approach is to use the special variable DET in conjunction with the INV function. For example, the statements

```
40   MAT   B=INV(A)
50   LET   A1=DET
```

would store the value of the determinant of matrix A in the simple variable A1. Another approach is to use an optional second argument in the INT function. This second argument is a simple variable whose value is the determinant calculated during execution of the INV function. For example, the statement

```
40   MAT   B=INV(A,A1)
```

would accomplish the same result as the previous example.

Files. Use of matrix statements to read from and write into files is available on several systems. These are generally direct extensions of the regular read and write statements for files. The extensions are generally analogous to the extension of the regular READ and PRINT statements to MAT READ and MAT PRINT.

8-7. In Summary

Since the use of vector notation is becoming increasingly more common in the scientific community, MAT statements provide the easiest route to programming more and more problems. The following exercises can be most readily programmed using these statements.

Exercises

For the ensuing exercises, use the following values of **A**, **B**, **C**, **D**, and **x**:

$$\mathbf{A} = \begin{bmatrix} 0 & 1 & 0 \\ 0 & 0 & 1 \\ -6 & -11 & -6 \end{bmatrix}$$

$$\mathbf{B} = \begin{bmatrix} 0 & 1 & 1 \\ 1 & 2 & 4 \\ 0 & 2 & 1 \end{bmatrix}$$

$$\mathbf{C} = \begin{bmatrix} 1 & 0 & 1 \\ 2 & -1 & 2 \\ 4 & 0 & -3 \end{bmatrix}$$

$$\mathbf{D} = \begin{bmatrix} 1 & 2 & 4 \\ -2 & 0 & 5 \\ 7 & 1 & 7 \end{bmatrix}$$

$$\mathbf{x} = \begin{bmatrix} 2 \\ -1 \\ 1 \end{bmatrix}$$

We shall use the notation $\mathbf{A}'$ to denote the transpose of $\mathbf{A}$.

8-1. Write a program to verify that for the square matrix $\mathbf{A}$ given above, the sum $\mathbf{A} + \mathbf{A}'$ is *symmetric* (i.e., $a_{ji} = a_{ij}$).

8-2. Write a program to verify that for the square matrix $\mathbf{A}$ given above, the difference $\mathbf{A} - \mathbf{A}'$ is *skew* symmetric (i.e., $a_{ji} = -a_{ij}$).

†8-3. Write a program to verify that the inverse of the symmetric matrix $(\mathbf{A} + \mathbf{A}')$ is also symmetric.

8-4. An orthogonal matrix is one that satisfies the relationship

$$\mathbf{X}^{-1} = \mathbf{X}'$$

Verify that the matrix

$$\mathbf{X} = \begin{bmatrix} \cos\theta & -\sin\theta \\ \sin\theta & \cos\theta \end{bmatrix}$$

is orthogonal for $\theta = 20°$.

8-5. For the matrix given above, verify that

$$(\mathbf{A}^{-1})' = (\mathbf{A}')^{-1}$$

8-6. For the matrices $\mathbf{A}$ and $\mathbf{B}$ given above, verify that

$$\mathbf{A} + \mathbf{B} = \mathbf{B} + \mathbf{A}$$

8-7. For the matrices $\mathbf{A}$ and $\mathbf{B}$ given above, verify that

$$(\mathbf{A} + \mathbf{B})' = \mathbf{A}' + \mathbf{B}'$$

†8-8. For the matrices $\mathbf{A}$ and $\mathbf{B}$ given above, verify that

$$\mathbf{A} * \mathbf{B} \neq \mathbf{B} * \mathbf{A}$$

8-9. For the matrices $\mathbf{A}$, $\mathbf{B}$, and $\mathbf{C}$ given above, verify that

$$(\mathbf{A} * \mathbf{B}) * \mathbf{C} = \mathbf{A} * (\mathbf{B} * \mathbf{C})$$

8-10. For the matrices $\mathbf{A}$, $\mathbf{B}$, $\mathbf{C}$, and $\mathbf{D}$ given above, verify that

$$(\mathbf{A} + \mathbf{B}) * (\mathbf{C} + \mathbf{D}) = \mathbf{A} * \mathbf{C} + \mathbf{A} * \mathbf{D} + \mathbf{B} * \mathbf{C} + \mathbf{B} * \mathbf{D}$$

8-11. Verify that the product $\mathbf{T}^{-1}\mathbf{A}\mathbf{T}$ is a diagonal matrix for $\mathbf{A}$ given above and for

$$\mathbf{T} = \begin{bmatrix} 1 & 1 & 1 \\ -1 & -2 & -3 \\ 1 & 4 & 9 \end{bmatrix}$$

8-12. For **A** and **B** given above and for **T** given by the previous exercise, verify that

$$\mathbf{B^{-1}T^{-1}ATB}$$

is a diagonal matrix.

INTRINSIC FUNCTIONS

SIN(x)	Trigonometric sine, x in radians
COS(x)	Trigonometric cosine, x in radians
TAN(x)	Trigonometric tangent, x in radians
ASN(x)	Angle (in radians) whose trigonometric sine is x
ACS(x)	Angle (in radians) whose trigonometric cosine is x
ATN(x)	Angle (in radians) whose trigonometric tangent is x
HTN(x)	Hyperbolic tangent, x in radians
EXP(x)	Natural exponent of x (e^x)
ABS(x)	Absolute value of x ($|x|$)
LOG(x)	Natural (base e) logarithm of x ($\ln x$)
LGT(x) or CLG(x)	Common (base 10) logarithm of x ($\log x$)
SQR(x)	Square root of x ($\sqrt{x}$)
INT(x)	Integral part of x
SGN(x)	Sign of x, defined as:

$$\text{if } x < 0, \text{ SGN }(x) = -1$$
$$\text{if } x = 0, \text{ SGN }(x) = 0$$
$$\text{if } x > 0, \text{ SGN }(x) = +1$$

AMERICAN STANDARD FLOW-CHART SYMBOLS‡

Any text or notes may be placed inside or beside these symbols.

Basic Input-Output Symbol (Represents an input or output operation if one of the special symbols is not used)

Communication Link (direct connection between remote locations)

Punched-card Input or Output

Processing Symbol (arithmetic operations)

Magnetic Tape Input or Output

Decision Symbol

Punched Paper Tape Input or Output

Predefined Process (Subroutine)

Printed Output (Document)

Manual Operation

Manual Input (Keyboard)

Auxiliary Operation of Off-line Equipment

Display Output (Video Devices, etc.)

Direction of Flow (with or without arrowheads)

Connector or Junction (to be used when the flow direction is broken)

On-line Storage (Magnetic Drums, Discs, etc.)

Terminal Symbol (Stop or Start)

Off-line Storage

Annotation Symbol (can be used to annotate the flow chart with additional comments)

‡These symbols are substantially those recommended by the X6 Committee to the United States of America Standards Institute, New York City.

SOLUTIONS TO SELECTED EXERCISES

Chapter 2

2-1. (a) (A+B)/(C+D)

(d) A*B/(C+10)

2-2. (b) (A+B)/(C+D/E)

(e) A/B+C*D/(E*F*G)

2-3. (d) (P*R/S)↑(T-1)

2-4. (b) LET X = -1/(2*A)+SIN(A/2)

(f) LET X = Y*SIN(3.1416/Z)

2-5. (b) LET X = ABS((1+COS(Y))/(1-COS(Y)))

(e) LET X = LGT(ABS(TAN(Y)))

2-6. (b) LET X = SQR(Y)*Z↑(I+1)*EXP(-Y)

(f) LET X = LGT(1/SQR(COS(Y)))*LGT(ABS(EXP(-X)))

2-8.‡ LIST

```
     AUG 24 15:43

     10 READ V
     20 LET G = 7.48*V
     30 PRINT G, "GALLONS"
     40 PRINT 28.316*V, "LITERS"
     50 PRINT V/27, "CUBIC YARDS"
     60 PRINT V*0.8036, "BUSHELS"
     70 PRINT G/31.5, "BARRELS"
     80 DATA 10
     99999 END

    >RUN
     74.8            GALLONS
```

‡See note on p. 4 to explain use of 0 and Ø.

```
283.16            LITERS
0.37037           CUBIC YARDS
8.036             BUSHELS
2.3746            BARRELS

>
```

2-14. LIST

```
   AUG 24 15:45

10 READ N,A,D
20 LET S=N*(2*A+(N-1)*D)/2
30 PRINT "SUM IS"S
40 DATA 20,1.5,2
99999 END

>RUN
SUM IS 410

>
```

2-20. LIST

```
   AUG 24 15:47

10 READ X,Y
20 REM CØNVERT X AND Y TØ RADIANS
30 LET X=X/57.3
40 LET Y=Y/57.3
50 LET L = SIN(X)+SIN(Y)
60 PRINT "LEFT SIDE =" L
70 LET R = 2*SIN((X+Y)/2)*CØS((X-Y)/2)
80 PRINT "RIGHT SIDE =" R
90 DATA 30,50
99999 END

>RUN
LEFT SIDE = 1.26604
RIGHT SIDE = 1.26604

>
```

2-26. LIST

```
   AUG 24 15:49

10 READ H,B
20 LET R = SQR(4*H*H+B*B)
30 LET L = R+B*B*LOG((2*H+R)/B)/(2*H)
40 LET A = 4*B*H/3
50 PRINT "LENGTH OF ARC IS" L
```

```
60 PRINT "AREA IS" A
70 DATA 6,3
99999 END

>RUN
LENGTH OF ARC IS 13.9404
AREA IS 24

>
```

Chapter 3

3-5. LIST

```
AUG 24 15:52

10 PRINT "PURCHASER","BILL"
20 READ P,U
30 IF U>300 THEN 80
40 IF U>100 THEN 100
50 LET B=U*1.75
60 PRINT P,B
70 GOTO 20
80 LET B=175+200*1.75*.9+(U-300)*1.75*.7
90 GOTO 60
100 LET B=175+(U-100)*1.75*.9
110 GOTO 60
120 DATA 177,75,201,398,141,147,102,181
99999 END

>RUN
PURCHASER          BILL
  177               131.25
  201               610.05
  141               249.025
  102               302.575

OUT OF DATA  20
```

3-12. LIST

```
AUG 24 15:56

10 READ B,I,P
20 LET N=0
30 LET K=I/100+1
40 LET B=B*K
50 IF B<P THEN 90
60 LET N=N+1
70 LET B=B-P
80 GOTO 40
```

```
90 PRINT "NUMBER OF FULL PAYMENTS",N
100 PRINT "FINAL PAYMENT", B
110 DATA 200, 1.5, 10
99999 END

>RUN
NUMBER OF FULL PAYMENTS          23
FINAL PAYMENT    9.56535

>
```

3-18. LIST

```
    AUG 24 16:00

10 LET N=0
15 LET R=10
20 LET D=INT(R/7)
30 PRINT D
40 LET N=N+1
50 LET R=(R-D*7)*10
60 IF N<20 THEN 20
99999 END

>RUN
 1
 4
 2
 8
 5
 7
 1
 4
 2
 8
 5
 7
 1
 4
 2
 8
 5
 7
 1
 4

>
```

3-23. LIST

```
    AUG 24 16:02

10 READ A
```

```
    20 LET N=0
    30 LET N=N+1
    40 LET A=(A+2)/(A+1)
    50 PRINT A
    60 IF N<10 THEN 30
    70 DATA 10
    99999 END

    >RUN
     1.09091
     1.47826
     1.40351
     1.41606
     1.4139
     1.41427
     1.4142
     1.41422
     1.41421
     1.41421

     >
```

3-30. LIST

```
    AUG 24 16:03

    10 READ A1, B1, C1, A2, B2, C2
    20 LET R=B2*A1-B1*A2
    30 IF R=0 THEN 80
    40 LET X=(C1*B2-C2*B1)/R
    50 LET Y=(A1*C2-A2*C1)/R
    60 PRINT "X=" X, "Y=" Y
    70 GOTO 10
    80 PRINT "NO SOLUTION"
    90 GOTO 10
    100 DATA 3,2,4,1,1,7
    99999 END

    >RUN
    X=-10            Y= 17

    OUT OF DATA  10

    >
```

Chapter 4

4-5. LIST

```
    AUG 24 16:04

    10 READ N
```

```
20 LET F=1
30 IF N=0 THEN 70
40 FOR I=1 TO N
50 LET F=F*I
60 NEXT I
70 PRINT N"FACTORIAL IS" F
80 DATA 8
99999 END

>RUN
  8 FACTORIAL IS 40320

>
```

4-10. LIST

```
    APR  9 20:20

10 READ N
20 PRINT "THE BINOMIAL COEFFICIENTS FOR N = "N
30 PRINT
40 PRINT "N","J","COEFFICIENT"
50 LET C=1
60 PRINT N,0,C
70 FOR J=1 TO N
80 LET C=C*(N-J+1)/J
90 PRINT N,J,C
100 NEXT J
110 DATA 8
99999 END

> RUN
THE BINOMIAL COEFFICIENTS FOR N =  8
```

N	J	COEFFICIENT
8	0	1
8	1	8
8	2	28
8	3	56
8	4	70
8	5	56
8	6	28
8	7	8
8	8	1

4-15. LIST

```
    AUG 24 16:06

10 LET A=0
20 READ N
30 LET D=2/N
40 LET X=D/2
```

```
 50 FOR I=1 TO N
 60 LET A=A+(1+X*X)*D
 70 LET X=X+D
 80 NEXT I
 90 PRINT N,A
100 GOTO 10
110 DATA 4,10,20,50,100,1000
99999 END
```

```
>RUN
  4                4.625
 10                4.66
 20          "     4.665
 50                4.6664
100                4.6666
1000               4.66667
```

```
OUT OF DATA  20
```

>

Chapter 5

5-5. LIST

```
AUG 24 16:11
```

```
10 READ N
20 FOR J=1 TO 5
30 LET I=.02*J
40 LET K=(I+1)↑N
50 LET F(J)=I*K/(K-1)
60 NEXT J
65 PRINT "N ="N
70 PRINT F(1),F(2),F(3),F(4),F(5)
80 GOTO 10
90 DATA 1,5,7,12
99999 END
```

```
>RUN
N = 1
  1.02        1.04        1.06        1.08        1.1
N = 5
  0.21216     0.22463     0.2374      0.25046     0.2638
N = 7
  0.15451     0.16661     0.17914     0.19207     0.20541
N = 12
  0.09456     0.10655     0.11928     0.1327      0.14676
```

```
OUT OF DATA  10
```

>

5-10. LIST

```
AUG 24 16:16

10 FOR I=1 TO 5
20 FOR J=1 TO 4
30 READ T(I,J)
40 NEXT J
50 NEXT I
60 PRINT "EXAM", "AVERAGE"
70 FOR J=1 TO 4
80 LET S=0
90 FOR I=1 TO 5
100 LET S=S+T(I,J)
110 NEXT I
120 PRINT J, S/5
130 NEXT J
140 PRINT
150 PRINT "STUDENT", "AVERAGE"
160 LET T=0
170 FOR I=1 TO 5
180 LET S=0
190 FOR J=1 TO 4
200 LET S=S+T(I,J)
210 NEXT J
220 LET T=T+S
230 PRINT I, S/4
240 NEXT I
250 PRINT
260 PRINT "AVERAGE ON ALL TESTS", T/20
270 DATA 48.6,30,62.8,23.4
280 DATA 40.1,40,60.1,29.6
290 DATA 63.4,50,63.7,31.2
300 DATA 56.2,60,58.2,27.3
310 DATA 71.0,70,67.3,26.4
99999 END

>RUN
EXAM            AVERAGE
 1              55.86
 2              50
 3              62.42
 4              27.58

STUDENT         AVERAGE
 1              41.2
 2              42.45
 3              52.075
 4              50.425
 5              58.675

AVERAGE ON ALL TESTS        48.967

>
```

5-15. LIST

```
     AUG 24 16:23

    10 READ N,C,D
    20 FOR I=1 TO N+1
    30 READ A(I)
    40 NEXT I
    50 PRINT "POWER OF X", "COEFFICIENT"
    60 PRINT 0, D*A(1)
    70 FOR P=1 TO N
    80 PRINT P, D*A(P+1)+C*A(P)
    90 NEXT P
    100 PRINT N+1, C*A(N+1)
    110 DATA 5,1.7,2.1
    120 DATA 0.8,6.1,0.2,-0.7,1.6,1
    99999 END

    >RUN
    POWER OF X        COEFFICIENT
      0                 1.68
      1                14.17
      2                10.79
      3                -1.13
      4                 2.17
      5                 4.82
      6                 1.7

    >
```

5-21. LIST

```
     APR 15 21:07
    10 DIM F(20)
    15 REM CALCULATE FUNCTION AND LOCATE LARGEST VALUE
    20 LET M=0
    30 FOR J=0 TO 10
    40 LET X=.1*J
    45 LET K=J+1
    50 LET F(K)=X↑2*SIN(3.1416*X)
    60 IF F(K)<=M THEN 80
    70 LET M=F(J)
    80 NEXT J
    85 REM OUTPUT SECTION
    90 PRINT "F(X) = X↑2 * SIN(3.1416*X)"
    100 PRINT
    110 PRINT "X","F(X)","NOR F(X)"
    120 FOR J=0 TO 10
    125 LET K=J+1
    130 PRINT .1*J,F(K),F(K)/M
    140 NEXT J
    99999 END
```

```
> RUN
F(X) = X↑2 * SIN(3.1416*X)
```

X	F(X)	NOR F(X)
0	0	0
0.1	3.09E-03	7.8E-03
0.2	0.02351	0.05931
0.3	0.07281	0.18367
0.4	0.15217	0.38386
0.5	0.25	0.63065
0.6	0.34238	0.86369
0.7	0.39642	1
0.8	0.37618	0.94895
0.9	0.2503	0.6314
1	-7.34639E-06	-1.8532E-05

Chapter 6

6-6. LIST

```
APR 15 21:54

10 DIM A$(10),N(10),T(10)
20 REM READ USER NAMES AND CHARGE NUMBERS
30 FOR J=1 TO 10
40 READ A$(J),N(J)
45 LET T(J)=0
50 NEXT J
60 REM READ TIMES
70 LET S=0
80 READ U,M
90 IF U=0 THEN 170
100 FOR J=1 TO 10
110 IF U=N(J) THEN 140
120 NEXT J
130 STOP
140 LET T(J)=T(J)+M
150 LET S=S+M
160 GOTO80
170 PRINT "USER","CHARGE NO","TIME USED","PER CENT"
180 FOR J=1 TO 10
190 IF T(J)=0 THEN 210
200 PRINT A$(J),N(J),T(J),T(J)*100/S
210 NEXT J
220 DATA "JOHN ANDERSON",70206
230 DATA "FRANK WILSON",40709
240 DATA "JOE EAST",50200
250 DATA "MYRON JOHNSON",40201
260 DATA "JACK EVERS",40710
270 DATA "HENRY WILLIAMS", 70207
280 DATA "JOHN SMITH",80001
```

```
290 DATA "MICHAEL SAND",50201
300 DATA "RALPH BLUE",70208
310 DATA "HORACE WHITE",40711
320 DATA 40709,1.27,80001,2.34,50200,2.11,40709,4.02,40201,3.11
330 DATA 70207,2.06,50200,3.09,80001,1.02,40709,0.79,70207,3.04
335 DATA 0,0
340 END
```

```
> RUN
USER                 CHARGE NO        TIME USED        PER CENT
FRANK WILSON         40709             6.08            26.6083
JOE EAST             50200             5.2             22.7571
MYRON JOHNSON        40201             3.11            13.6105
HENRY WILLIAMS       70207             5.1             22.3195
JOHN SMITH           80001             3.36            14.7046
```

6-11. LIST

```
APR 15 21:21

10 PRINT TAB(22);"CAPITAL RECOVERY FACTOR"
20 PRINT "PERCENT";
30 LET K=12
40 FOR J=2 TO 10 STEP 2
50 PRINT TAB(K);J;
60 K=K+10
70 NEXT J
80 PRINT
90 PRINT "YEAR";
100 LET K=13
110 FOR J=1 TO 5
120 PRINT TAB(K);"**";
125 LET K=K+10
130 NEXT J
140 PRINT
150 READ N
160 FOR J=1 TO N
170 PRINT J;TAB(5);"*";
180 LET T=10
190 FOR I=.02 TO .1 STEP .02
200 LET C=(I+1)↑J
210 LET C=I*C/(C-1)
220 LET C=INT(C*1E4+.5)/1E4
230 PRINT TAB(T);C;
240 LET T=T+10
250 NEXT I
260 PRINT
270 NEXT J
280 DATA 15
99999 END
```

```
> RUN
```

CAPITAL RECOVERY FACTOR

PERCENT		2	4	6	8	10
YEAR		**	**	**	**	**
1	*	1.02	1.04	1.06	1.08	1.1
2	*	0.515	0.5302	0.5454	0.5608	0.5762
3	*	0.3468	0.3603	0.3741	0.388	0.4021
4	*	0.2626	0.2755	0.2886	0.3019	0.3155
5	*	0.2122	0.2246	0.2374	0.2505	0.2638
6	*	0.1785	0.1908	0.2034	0.2163	0.2296
7	*	0.1545	0.1666	0.1791	0.1921	0.2054
8	*	0.1365	0.1485	0.161	0.174	0.1874
9	*	0.1225	0.1345	0.147	0.1601	0.1736
10	*	0.1113	0.1233	0.1359	0.149	0.1627
11	*	0.1022	0.1141	0.1268	0.1401	0.154
12	*	0.0946	0.1066	0.1193	0.1327	0.1468
13	*	0.0881	0.1001	0.113	0.1265	0.1408
14	*	0.0826	0.0947	0.1076	0.1213	0.1357
15	*	0.0778	0.0899	0.103	0.1168	0.1315

6-16. APR 20 21:52

```
10 READ N
20 READ A
30 PRINT "(";A;") X↑";N;" + "
40 LET N=N-1
50 IF N>1 THEN 20
60 READ A
70 PRINT "(";A;") X        + "
80 READ A
90 PRINT "(";A;")"
100 DATA 3,1.217,1.798,-4.102,9.17
99999 END

> RUN
( 1.217 ) X↑ 3   +
( 1.798 ) X↑ 2   +
(-4.102 ) X       +
( 9.17 )
```

Chapter 7

7-3. LIST

AUG 24 16:24

```
10 DEF FNS(X)=ATN(X/SQR(!9)*57.3
20 READ A
30 PRINT "X","ARCSIN(X)"
40 PRINT A,FNS(A)
50 DATA 0.726
99999 END
```

```
>RUN
X                    ARCSIN(X)
 0.726                54.2122


>6
```

7-7. LIST

```
   AUG 24 16:27

10 DEF FNF(X)=X*X*(4*X-1)+LOG(X)/X
20 READ X
30 LET F1=FNF(X)
40 READ H
50 PRINT H,(FNF(X+H)-F1)/H
60 GOTO40
70 DATA 4,0.001,0.01,0.1
99999 END

>RUN
 1E-03               184.023
 0.01                202.943
 0.1                 210.059

OUT OF DATA   40

>
```

7-12. LIST

```
   AUG 24 16:30

10 READ A
20 GOSUB 50
30 PRINT A,S
40 STOP
50 IF A>1 THEN 80
60 LET S=ATN(A/SQR(1-A))*57.3
70 RETURN
80 PRINT "ARCSIN("A;") DOES NOT EXIST"
90 STOP
100 DATA 0.726
99999 END

>RUN
 0.726               54.2122

>
```

Chapter 8

8-3. (a) Program for systems that do not recognize zero subscripts

```
LIST

   AUG 24 16:31

10 DIM A(5,5), B(5,5)
20 MAT READ A(2,2)
30 MAT B=ZER(2,2)
40 MAT B=TRN(A)
50 MAT B=A+B
60 MAT A=INV(B)
70 MAT PRINT A
80 DATA 0,1,0,0,0,1,-6,-11,-6
99999 END

>RUN
-0.75758            0.54545          -0.07576

 0.54545           -0.27273          -0.04545

-0.07576           -0.04545          -7.58E-03


>
```

(b) Program for systems that recognize zero subscripts

```
LIST

   AUG 24 16:33

10 DIM A(5,5), B(5,5)
20 MAT READ A(3,3)
30 MAT B=ZER(3,3)
40 MAT B=TRN(A)
50 MAT B=A+B
60 MAT A=INV(B)
70 MAT PRINT A
80 DATA 0,1,0,0,0,1,-6,-11,-6
99999 END

>
```

8-8.   (a) Program for systems that do not recognize zero subscripts

```
LIST

   AUG 24 16:38

10 DIM A(5,5), B(5,5), C(5,5)
20 MAT READ A(3,3), B(3,3)
30 MAT C=ZER(3,3)
```

```
40 MAT C=A*B
50 PRINT "A*B"
60 MAT PRINT C
70 PRINT
75 PRINT "B*A"
80 MAT C=B*A
90 MAT PRINT C
100 DATA 0,1,0,0,0,1,-6,-11,-6
110 DATA 0,1,1,1,2,4,0,2,1
99999 END

>
```

(b) Program for systems that recognize zero subscripts

```
>LIST

 AUG 24 16:36

10 DIM A(5,5), B(5,5), C(5,5)
20 MAT READ A(2,2), B(2,2)
30 MAT C=ZER(2,2)
40 MAT C=A*B
50 PRINT "A*B"
60 MAT PRINT C
70 PRINT
75 PRINT "B*A"
80 MAT C=B*A
90 MAT PRINT C
100 DATA 0,1,0,0,0,1,-6,-11,-6
110 DATA 0,1,1,1,2,4,0,2,1
99999 END

>RUN
A*B
 1              2              4

 0              2              1

-11            -40            -56


B*A
-6             -11            -5

-24            -43            -22

-6             -11            -4


>
```

INDEX

Printer and Binder: Malloy Lithographing, Inc.
82 83 84   9 8 7 6 5